Collins

Social Studies
Atlas
for Jamaica

SECONDARY
WORKBOOK

Series editor: **Farah Christian**

Collins

William Collins' dream of knowledge for all began with the publication of his first book in 1819. A self-educated mill worker, he not only enriched millions of lives, but also founded a flourishing publishing house. Today, staying true to this spirit, Collins books are packed with inspiration, innovation and practical expertise. They place you at the centre of a world of possibility and give you exactly what you need to explore it.

Collins. Freedom to teach.

Published by Collins
An imprint of HarperCollins*Publishers*
Westerhill Road, Bishopbriggs, Glasgow, G64 2QT

HarperCollins Publishers
Macken House, 39/40 Mayor Street Upper, Dublin 1, D01 C9W8, Ireland

Browse the complete Collins Caribbean catalogue at
www.collins.co.uk/caribbeanschools

© HarperCollins*Publishers* Limited 2019

Maps © Collins Bartholomew Limited and Mona Informatix Limited 2018

10 9 8 7 6 5 4

ISBN 978-0-00-836173-0

Series editor: Farah Christian
Author: Naam Thomas
Publisher: Dr Elaine Higgleton
Project manager: Julianna Dunn
Copy editor: Mitch Fitton
Proofreader: Helen Bleck
Typesetter: QBS Learning
Cover image: Photo Spirit/Shutterstock; Danita Delmont/Shutterstock
Printed in United Kingdom

Acknowledgements
p7, 172: Ethan Daniels/Shutterstock, p7: Robert Fried/Alamy Stock Image, p20: Asma Samoh/Shutterstock, p20: LOOK Die Bildagentur der Fotografen GmbH/Alamy Stock Photo, p21: John de la Bastide/Shutterstock, p21: OkFoto/Shutterstock, p36: Ian Cumming/Getty Images, p36: National Geographic Creative/Alamy Stock Photo, p36: Education Images/Getty Images, p37: Michael Dwyer/Alamy Stock Images, p37: Sean Sprague/Alamy Stock Images, p37: CREATISTA/Shutterstock, p37: Ruth Peterkin/Shutterstock, p122: Kkulikov/Shutterstocl, p123: Tami Freed/Shutterstock, p125: Serg Zastavkin/Shutterstock, p170: Altan Osmanaj/Shutterstock, p173: Steve Photography/Shutterstock, p174: Ethan Daniels/Shutterstock, p175: Sven Creutzmann/Mambo photo/Getty Images, p176: Robin Moore/GettyImages

Contents

Introduction

This *Collins Jamaica Atlas for Social Studies Secondary Workbook* has been specially written to complement the *Collins Social Studies Atlas for Jamaica*. It contains activities that have been developed to meet the learning objectives relating to Jamaica and its geography, history, heritage, land use, environment and government in grades 7–9 of the National Standards Curriculum for Social Studies.

This workbook contains activities that will require students to apply what they learn, and also to analyse and evaluate data and to make deductive reasoning using the contents of the atlas, in line with the objectives of the curriculum. Some of the activities include students analysing and interpreting map information, analysing and creating statistical graphs and diagrams, drawing conclusions from maps and timelines, and writing summaries. Importantly, many of the activities in this workbook provide practice of the skills – such as using data presented to answer a specific question, extrapolating key information from that data, and explaining how the data helps to answer the question – that students need for progressing to CSEC® level. There is strong emphasis on identification of Jamaican examples and culturally relevant locations and concepts. Expansion of these concepts through comparison and contrast to Caribbean and international case studies encourages students to apply regional and global solutions to local problems.

We have also included activities that bring in **STEM** and **Extended Learning**:

- The **STEM activities** are ideas for projects that are designed to help students learn to apply scientific and mathematical principles to problems while using a range of tools, including digital resources. Through these activities, students will practise problem-solving and reflection on tasks completed.

- **Extended Learning activities** are designed to help students move beyond the atlas to explore other sources of information. These activities will create opportunities for students to carry out further research and to use a range of resources to gather information to complete the tasks. These activities cannot be directly completed using the atlas alone. However, they are tied directly to the curriculum units and may be assigned to students as homework.

- Research skills relevant to scaffolding CSEC®-level studies help students to plan and execute streamlined data collection and field study results presentation in a way that prepares them for the Social Studies and Geography SBA. Some activities related to vocabulary require the student to use the *Collins Jamaican School Dictionary*. If this dictionary is unavailable, any good dictionary may be used instead.

In some cases, we suggest that students carry out research online, and suggest some websites that students could use. Please make sure that all internet-based research is supervised to ensure that students are only accessing relevant sites, that students are only using the internet for research purposes and not for social media and emails, and to make sure that students are not in any way exposing themselves to risk. Please make sure that any internet-based research carried out in school is in line with school policy, and please encourage parents to supervise any internet-based research that is set as homework.

Grade 7 – Term 1, Unit 1

In this unit you will learn about what it means to be a **citizen**. We will also learn about the attitudes and behaviours of responsible citizens.

Citizenship is an important part of society. What citizenship means in each country may be different, and individuals may choose to exercise their citizenship in their own way. However, some things are universal: citizenship always involves access to **rights** and certain standards of living; citizens have **responsibilities** to themselves and to society; and citizenship must be **active** and practised for it to mean something.

---

1 Use the *Collins Jamaican School Dictionary* and other sources to define the following terms.

a) citizen

_____

b) dual citizenship

_____

c) active citizenship

_____

d) global citizenship

_____

e) digital citizenship

_____

f) economic citizenship

_____

g) naturalisation

_____

h) alien

_____

i) deportation

_____

j) rights

_____

k) responsibilities

_____

l) freedom

_____

2 Use the *Collins Jamaican School Dictionary* and other sources, such as the internet, to correctly complete the paragraphs below. Use the words provided in brackets at the end of each paragraph. Each word is to be used only once.

a) A good Jamaican citizen must have certain _____. These are attributes and personality traits that a citizen has and that help to guide his actions and _____. When a citizen does what is expected of him, this is called carrying out one's civic _____ or civic responsibility. **(attitudes, qualities, duty)**

b) A citizen should be honest, _____ the law and respect authority. This is important since laws _____ citizens. People in authority have _____ which helps them to guide others. For example, a student should obey teachers, policemen and their parents. **(experience, obey, protect)**

c) _____ to the community is also a sign of being a good citizen. This includes paying _____, and staying informed about current affairs. Taking care of the environment and _____ are also important. This shows that a citizen cares about _____, not only themselves. **(taxes, contributing, community, others)**

d) A citizen must perform their role in society to the best of their _____. A student should do their best in school to make the most of their _____. Each person has a part to play. **(ability, education)**

e) Supporting democracy by _____ is also a civic duty. A good citizen should also _____ in social and cultural events such as _____, to help promote the unique culture of Jamaica. **(festivals, participate, voting)**

f) A good citizen should also be a patriot. This means they show genuine _____ for their country. When a citizen works to improve their country, respects the national symbols and serves in the military, they are being _____. **(patriotic, love)**

g) A good citizen is also tolerant and respectful of others. A _____ only works when each person is allowed to _____ themselves and exercise their rights. It is important to respect each other's beliefs and traditions. This is especially important in a _____ society such as Jamaica. **(express, multicultural, society)**

3 Examine the image below, then respond to the questions that follow.

a) Describe the images.

_____

_____

b) Citizens have the right to a safe, healthy and sustainable environment and a responsibility to the public's interests. Reflect on this statement and explain two reasons why littering is not a behaviour of a good citizen.

_____

_____

_____

_____

c) How can a good citizen work with the community to fix the problems shown in the images?

_____

_____

d) How can a good citizen prevent the problems shown in the images before they happen?

_____

_____

e) The image on page 22 of the _Social Studies Atlas for Jamaica_ illustrates a problem in Belize. Why do good citizens need to care about what happens in other countries?

_____

_____

4 Examine the pie charts below from page 41 of the *Social Studies Atlas for Jamaica*, then respond to the questions that follow.

a) Complete the graphs by adding the missing figures, colouring the graphs and inserting the key and title.

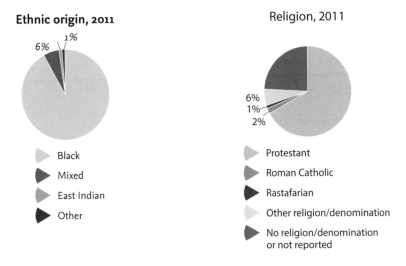

Ethnic origin, 2011
1%
6%

Black
Mixed
East Indian
Other

Religion, 2011
6%
1%
2%

Protestant
Roman Catholic
Rastafarian
Other religion/denomination
No religion/denomination or not reported

b) Which ethnic origins are the highest and the lowest percentage of Jamaica's population?

_____

c) Which religions have the highest and the lowest percentage of Jamaica's population?

_____

d) Every citizen, regardless of race, religion, place of origin, political opinions, colour, creed or sex, is entitled to freedom from discrimination. Reflect on this statement.

i) Use the *Collins Jamaican School Dictionary* to define the word 'discrimination'.

_____

_____

ii) Explain why you think discrimination can create problems in society.

_____

_____

iii) Suggest one way that you can help to stop discrimination in society.

_____

_____

e) Describe how a citizen might discriminate against another citizen based on:

i) race/ethnic origin

_____

_____

ii) political opinion

_____

_____

iii) religion

_____

_____

5 Examine the government structure diagram on page 24 of the *Social Studies Atlas for Jamaica*, and what each arm of government does. State one way in which each arm of government may help to protect the citizens of Jamaica.

a) The Legislature

_____

_____

b) The Executive

_____

_____

c) The Judiciary

_____

_____

6 **a)** **Extended Learning:** conduct research to find out two ways a person from another country could become a Jamaican citizen.

_____

_____

b) **Extended Learning:** conduct online research to find out the four core principles of the Convention on the Rights of the Child.

_____

_____

_____

_____

Grade 7 – Term 1, Unit 2

In this unit you will learn about the **National Heroes** of Jamaica and their roles as nation builders.

The **National Heroes** of Jamaica played an invaluable role in the development of the country. To do this they had to exhibit qualities that allowed them to make the most of their individual talents and resources in ways that benefited others.

1 Use the *Collins Jamaican School Dictionary* and other sources to complete the concept map below by filling in the definitions of the terms in each box.

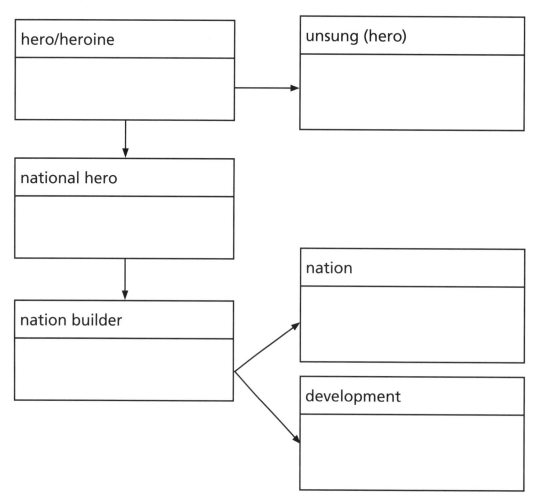

2 Each word below is a quality a hero must have. Use the *Collins Jamaican School Dictionary* to help you with the meaning of the words listed. Then match each word a)–j) with the correct definition i)–x).

a)	supportive	**i)**	the quality shown by people who do things knowing they are dangerous or difficult
b)	selfless	**ii)**	expressing very strong feelings about something
c)	passionate	**iii)**	the quality of following your principles
d)	courage	**iv)**	truthful and trustworthy
e)	care	**v)**	someone who is sure of their own abilities or qualities
f)	integrity	**vi)**	the ability to be tolerant and stay calm in a difficult situation
g)	patience	**vii)**	putting other people's interests before your own
h)	honest	**viii)**	concern or worry, looking after something or someone
i)	humility	**ix)**	the quality of being modest and humble
j)	confident	**x)**	encouraging and helpful to someone who is in difficulties

3 Seven individuals have been honoured as National Heroes of Jamaica. Their heroic acts show the qualities of a hero listed above. Read pages 42–43 in the *Social Studies Atlas for Jamaica* to complete the following exercise.

a) Paul Bogle led protests to end poverty and social injustice. How did this show that Paul Bogle was passionate about these two social issues?

_____

_____

b) Paul Bogle's heroism paved the way for just treatment of people in the courts. Explain why this showed that his actions were supportive.

_____

_____

c) Sir Alexander Bustamante began working to improve the pay and working conditions of people when Jamaica was still a British colony. Why would you call this a caring act?

_____

_____

d) Sir Alexander Bustamante founded the Jamaica Labour Party in 1943 and he became the first Prime Minister of independent Jamaica in 1962. How did this demonstrate his patience?

_____

_____

e) George William Gordon sold his land cheaply to freed slaves. Explain why this was an act of selflessness.

_____

_____

f) George William Gordon was a businessman, politician and landowner who worked with freed slaves. Explain why this demonstrated his humility.

_____

_____

g) Queen Nanny was a great Maroon leader and military strategist against the British during the First Maroon War from 1720 to 1739. Explain why this role required confidence.

_____

_____

h) Samuel Sharpe encouraged slaves to stand by their decision to refuse to work on Christmas Day unless their pleas for better treatment and freedom were considered. Why was this a courageous thing to do?

_____

_____

4 The Order of National Hero is the highest honour that may be given to a citizen of Jamaica. Read about the order on page 43 of the *Social Studies Atlas for Jamaica* then answer the questions below.

a) In what year was the Order of National Hero established?

_____

b) For someone to be given this award, he or she must have

_____.

c) What do you think the motto of the order, *'He built a city which hath foundations'* means?

_____

_____

5 For each famous Jamaican listed, read pages 42–43 in the *Social Studies Atlas for Jamaica* and use the internet to carry out some research to list one of their achievements. For each achievement, explain what heroic quality they demonstrated.

a) Usain Bolt

_____

_____

b) Bob Marley

_____

_____

c) Marlon James

_____

_____

d) Louise Bennett-Coverley

_____

_____

e) Ralston Miller 'Rex' Nettleford

_____

_____

6 Examine the timeline on page 42 and the description of each National Hero on page 43. Describe how some events and social issues may have influenced the actions of each National Hero.

a) What historical event could have influenced 'Queen Nanny' to become the great Maroon leader and military strategist she was?

_____

_____

b) In 1808 the Slave trade Abolition Bill was passed. This meant that it became illegal for persons to engage in the trade of enslaved people. How could this have influenced Samuel Sharpe to lead the 'Christmas Rebellion'?

_____

_____

c) **i)** What historical event happened in 1838?

_____

ii) What were the conditions like for people after this which caused the Morant Bay Rebellion led by Paul Bogle and influenced actions taken by George William Gordon?

_____

_____

d) **i)** Marcus Garvey founded the UNIA in 1914. How many years after this did he form the People's Political Party?

_____

ii) The People's Political Party was one of the first political parties founded in Jamaica. How may this have influenced the work of Norman Manley to found the People's National Party and Sir Alexander Bustamante to found the Jamaica Labour Party?

_____

_____

e) What were the conditions like for people in Jamaica that influenced the founding of the Jamaica Labour Party and People's National Party by Sir Alexander Bustamante and Norman Manley?

_____

_____

7 One way that the government honours our National Heroes is by naming places after them. Carry out some research and add locations and names of places in Jamaica named for the National Heroes to the following map. These places may be schools, roads, communities, buildings or National monuments.

Highway
Main road (A)
Main road (B)
Other road
Parish boundary

Scale 1 : 1 250 000

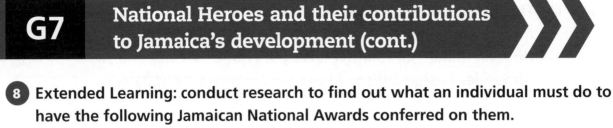

G7 National Heroes and their contributions to Jamaica's development (cont.)

8 **Extended Learning:** conduct research to find out what an individual must do to have the following Jamaican National Awards conferred on them.

a) Order of the Nation

_____

b) Order of Excellence

_____

c) Order of Merit

_____

d) Order of Jamaica

_____

e) Order of Distinction

_____

f) Badge of Honour

_____

g) Medal of Honour

_____

Grade 7 – Term 1, Unit 3

In this unit you will learn about the characteristics of **culture** and how parts of culture are classified. We will also learn about how culture is continued and preserved.

Culture is an important part of society because it is the way that each person in any society develops their **value** system. This in turn is a means for each person to regulate their behaviour and evaluate where they fit within that society and to develop an **identity**. Culture is experienced in everything from language to geography, history and art; therefore, it is impossible to escape cultural influences. It is the responsibility of the current generation to determine what the culture of future generations will be. This occurs through omitting, changing or maintaining certain **cultural traits** or practices, since culture is **learnt**.

1 Use the *Collins Jamaican School Dictionary* and other sources to define the following terms.

a) culture

_____

b) heritage

_____

c) ethnic group

_____

d) melting pot

_____

e) cultural heritage

_____

f) preservation

_____

Culture can be described as either material or non-material. Material culture is physical. It can be touched and therefore includes symbols, cultural buildings, heritage sites and objects used in traditions. Non-material culture is not physical. It must be learnt and practised and has to do with how people in a culture think about the world around them, others and themselves. This includes beliefs and value systems, norms and how traditions are carried out. For each image describe if an aspect of material or non-material culture is being shown, or both. Explain your answers.

a)

_____

_____

b)

_____

_____

c)

_____

_____

d)

_____

_____

Use the _Social Studies Atlas for Jamaica_ to locate the following images and complete the exercise.

e) Page 24: Jamaican ackee

_____

_____

f) Page 47: Junkanoo mask

_____

_____

g) Page 71: Mashramani dancer

_____

_____

h)   Page 33: St Mary Parish Church

_____

_____

i)   Page 58: Vincy Mas dancer

_____

_____

3   **a)**   Use the timeline on page 42 of the _Social Studies Atlas for Jamaica_ and other sources to create your own simple timeline showing the arrival of the various ethnic groups in Jamaica. Give your timeline an appropriate title.

    b)   Look at pages 20–21 in the _Social Studies Atlas for Jamaica_ and write the country of origin of each of the ethnic groups on your timeline in brackets next to the group.

4   **Extended Learning: conduct additional research to find out the ethnic group that originated each aspect of culture shown in each image. Briefly state if each aspect of culture shown should be maintained, discarded or changed. Give reasons for your answers.**

    a)   _____

_____

    b)   _____

_____

c) _____

_____

d) _____

_____

e) _____

_____

f) _____

_____

g) _____

_____

h) _____

_____

i) _____

_____

5 Extended Learning: work in groups to list five aspects of Jamaican culture that are important to you and your group members. These may include language, music, dance, traditions, buildings, customs, values, and natural or man-made heritage sites. Come up with a 'Culture Preservation Plan' which describes strategies and methods you would use so that the five parts of culture you chose could be preserved for future generations of Jamaicans. Present your plan to the class in an interesting and creative way.

Grade 7 – Term 2, Unit 1

In this unit you will learn about global, regional and local **natural resources**. We will also learn about resource management.

Natural resources are parts of the *environment* that humans cannot make but are necessary for human life as we know it. This is why resources must be managed since they can potentially be used up too quickly and no alternatives exist. They can only be replenished by *natural processes*. Additionally, methods of accessing and utilising some of these resources can be directly harmful to the environment or humans themselves and the impact of indirect problems such as *pollution* and some by-products cannot be ignored. In the Caribbean, access to natural resources is limited. Therefore, their *sustainable* use is important for our future development.

1 Use the *Collins Jamaican School Dictionary* and other sources to complete the concept map below by filling in the definitions of the terms in each box.

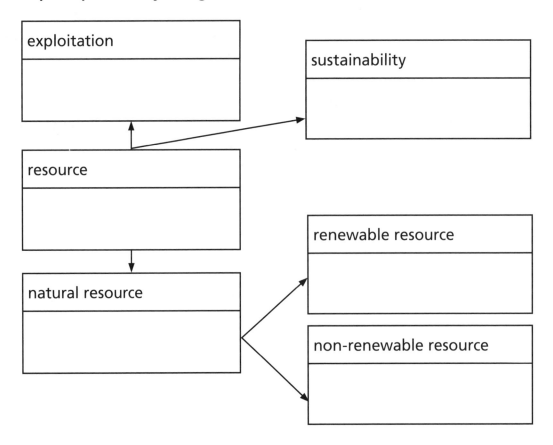

2 Vegetation is a natural resource. Plants are used to research new medicines, manufacture furniture, provide energy and heat homes when they become coal and firewood and to make timber that becomes useful buildings. Plants also affect the climate by releasing water into the atmosphere, they protect the soil by preventing erosion and provide habitat for wildlife. Around the world there are many different types of vegetation which are adapted to different temperatures, amounts of water and seasons. The main types of vegetation can be seen on page 97 of your *Social Studies Atlas for Jamaica*. Use the world vegetation map on page 97 of your *Social Studies Atlas for Jamaica* to complete the exercise below. Circle the correct answer from each set of choices.

a)   Which type of vegetation is located on the Equator?

   Arctic tundra   Tropical forest   Temperate grassland

b)   On which continent can we find the largest spread of Desert/Desert type vegetation?

   Africa   Australia   America

c)   Mountain/Alpine vegetation can be found on which South American coast?

   North coast   West coast   East coast

d)   Which type of vegetation is found in warm or hot climates and would be best for grazing livestock?

   Mediterranean   Coniferous forest   Savanna grassland

e)   Which type of forest receives the most rain?

   Boreal/Taiga forest   Tropical forest   Sub tropical forest

f)   Which type of vegetation is also called 'steppes'?

   Temperate grassland   Mediterranean   Mixed forest

g)   Plants that can survive very cold conditions would be found in the:

   Mixed forest   Monsoon forest   Arctic tundra

3 Use pages 100–101 in the *Social Studies Atlas for Jamaica* to answer the following questions about human impacts on forest resources.

a)   Define deforestation.

_____

b)   List two reasons why forests may be cleared.

_____

c) What are two other names for forest fires?

_____

d) What weather conditions do you think may cause forest fires?

_____

e) Describe two negative impacts of deforestation.

_____

_____

4 Examine the deforestation map on page 101 of the *Social Studies Atlas for Jamaica* then answer the questions below.

a) On which continent was there a decrease in forest cover by 4.8% between the year 2000 and 2010?

_____

b) On which continent was there no change in the forest cover during the same period?

_____

c) On which continent was there an increase in forest cover by 3.9?

_____

d) Compare all the continents. Between the year 2000 and 2010, was the increase in forest cover greater than the reduction in forest cover?

_____

5 Use the internet and other resources to find out about the following.

a) Why are forests important to prevent global warming?

_____

_____

b) What are two ways in which deforestation may be reduced?

_____

_____

6 **Use the Jamaica Industry, Minerals map on page 38 of the _Social Studies Atlas for Jamaica_ to complete the exercise.**

a) Complete the map below.

    i) Label each parish.

    ii) Shade the bauxite deposits and the bauxite mining areas using two different colours.

    iii) Insert the alumina processing plants.

    iv) Insert and label the bauxite ports.

    v) Insert the railways.

    vi) Add a compass rose and a key to your map. Remember that the key must show what each colour and symbol used represents.

    vii) Give your map an appropriate title.

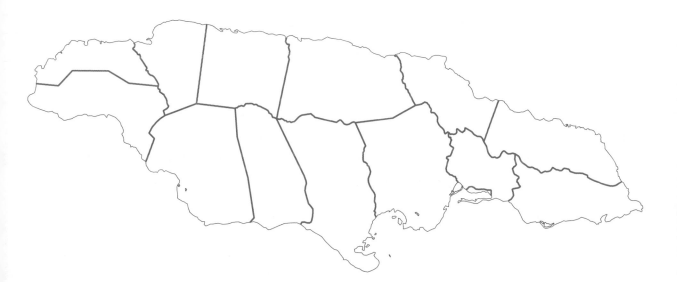

b) Name the four parishes with the largest bauxite deposits.

_____

c) List the four parishes with smaller bauxite deposits.

_____

d) List the four parishes where bauxite mining is located.

_____

e) Why do you think that all the bauxite deposits are not also bauxite mining areas?

_____

f) Why do you think a railroad is used to transport alumina and bauxite instead of roads?

_____

g) Look at the physical map on pages 26–27 and cross reference with the Industry, Minerals map on page 38 in the *Social Studies Atlas for Jamaica*.

i) List the 2 northern mountain ranges where bauxite deposits are located.

_____

ii) List the 5 southern mountain ranges where bauxite deposits are located.

_____

7 a) Use the Energy and Minerals map on page 18 of the *Social Studies Atlas for Jamaica* to identify the different mineral resources found across the Caribbean. List the minerals and the countries in which they are found.

Minerals	Countries

b) Present the information in the table on page 28 in a graphical form by using it to create a bar graph. Give your graph a title and complete with a key

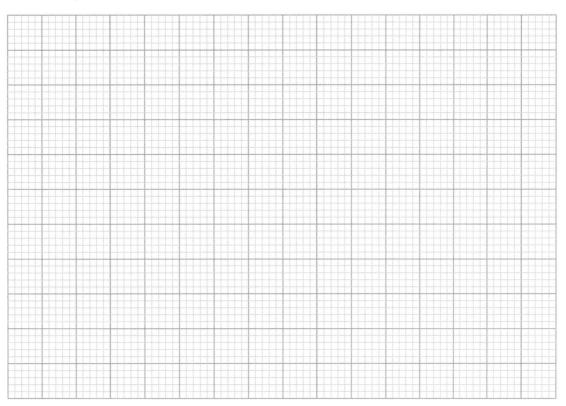

8 Use the Trinidad mining map on page 66 and Guyana minerals map on page 71 of the *Social Studies Atlas for Jamaica* to complete the exercise on the next page.

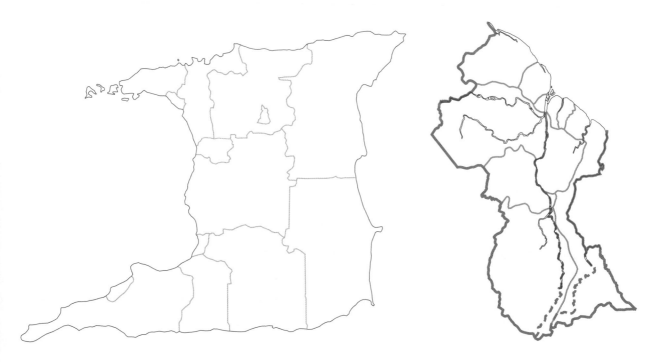

a) For each map:

   i)   shade the areas where the different mineral resources are found

   ii) insert the names of the different provinces/parishes

   iii) identify the capital city.

b) Comment on the distribution of these resources by describing where they are mainly found (inland, coastal area, close to rivers, in mountainous areas, scattered or close to each other).

_____

_____

_____

_____

_____

_____

9 **Fishing and forestry are considered part of Caribbean resources. Reflect on the fishing and forestry map and fish landings graph on page 18 of the *Social Studies Atlas for Jamaica* and then answer the following questions.**

a) Use the pie chart to complete the following.

   i)   Which Caribbean country has the largest percentage of fish landings?

   ii) Which Caribbean country has the smallest percentage of fish landings?

   iii) What is the difference percentage between the landings for Jamaica and the country with the largest percentage?

b) Complete the following using the map.

   i)   What do the blue lines on the map represent?

   ii) On the map on the next page identify the countries listed in the pie chart on fish landings, shade them and insert the figures from the graph. Draw lines to show the EEZ boundaries for each. Complete with a key and title.

c) Use the *Collins Jamaica School Dictionary* and other resources to help complete the following tasks.

i) Explain why fishing and forestry are considered natural resources.

_____

ii) Explain if fishing and forestry are renewable or non-renewable resources.

_____

iii) Describe one threat to forestry resources in the Caribbean.

_____

iv) Describe one threat to fishing resources in the Caribbean.

_____

v) Describe one way Caribbean forestry resources can be protected.

_____

vi) Describe one way Caribbean fishing resources can be protected.

_____

10 **Extended Learning: Case study Bauxite Mining in Jamaica – The Growth of Mandeville**

a) Examine the Industry, Minerals map on page 38 of the *Social Studies Atlas for Jamaica* and shade the areas of bauxite deposits and bauxite mining in Manchester parish.

b) Read the extract and use page 29 of the *Social Studies Atlas for Jamaica* to complete the exercise.

Development and Boundaries of Mandeville

Today Manchester produces a large amount of Jamaica's Irish potato crop and is also noted for its high-quality production of citrus, bananas and ground provisions; dairy farming also takes place. The parish is still known for producing coffee, particularly through the High Mountain Coffee Factory located in Williamsfield. Bauxite is mined on a large scale and much of Mandeville's development and economic prosperity is owed to this mineral as the bauxite companies had invested greatly in the development of Manchester. In the 1900s, Mandeville's population increased as a result of the number of foreign experts and Jamaicans in the bauxite field migrating to Manchester. Hundreds of persons from Kingston were also employed by the bauxite companies and naturally became Mandeville residents. In 1957, the establishment of the alumina mining company, Alcan Bauxite, caused a population explosion and in the 1960s, Alcan and Kaiser bauxite companies employed well over 3,000 persons. As a result of this, Mandeville has been described as a town which grew on bauxite.

The Mandeville urban and urbanising area has spread from its early 19th-century centre over an extensive area of the central Manchester Plateau. The approximate boundaries run from Hanbury and Clark's Town in the north to Knockpatrick and Ellen Street in the south and from Royal Flat in the east to Dunsinane in the west.

Source: National Library of Jamaica. (ND). 'History of Manchester'. Retrieved February 27, 2019, from https://www.nlj.gov.jm/history-notes/History%20 of%20Manchester.pdf

Manchester Parish Development Committee https://manchesterpdc.files. wordpress.com/2011/03/16da-3-mandeville-profile-long.pdf Retrieved February 27, 2019.

i) On the map of Manchester show the growth of Mandeville from the 1900s until now. Use different colours to illustrate the size of Mandeville at different time periods. Include a descriptive key.

MANCHESTER

Mandeville

ii) Shade the map to predict future growth of Mandeville.

c) Describe three ways in which the bauxite industry influenced the growth of Mandeville.

_____

_____

_____

_____

_____

_____

11 a) Use page 25 of the *Social Studies Atlas for Jamaica* and the clues provided to complete the crossword.

Across

2. This word describes most of the Cockpit Country.
7. One of the types of rock that forms the central uplands.
8. The Cockpit Country is made of this type of rock.
9. Located on Jamaica's coastal zone.

Down

1. This water resource is also important to Jamaica.
3. Rivers in the south of Jamaica are important resources to this industry.
4. This industry depends on the sea as a water resource.
5. This industry depends on the sun and sea as resources.
6. Wetlands protect the shoreline from this process.
10. Rainforests depend on this resource along with water and soil.

b) **Extended Learning:** do some research on the internet to write a short paragraph explaining why you think the sun, sea and land are important resources to Jamaica.

Grade 7 – Term 2, Unit 2

In this unit you will learn about **human resources** and **industrial activity**.

Human resources are the people that make industries work. Human resources are important to transform natural resources from **raw materials** to **finished products**, a key part of increasing **profitability**, and getting products into the hands of consumers. Human **intellect** is itself also a resource. Therefore, some industries are entirely dependent on knowledge and research, for example software development. Human resources also require management since **education** and **experience** must be properly placed and directed for best application of workers' **skills**.

1 Use the *Collins Jamaican School Dictionary* and other sources to define the following terms.

a) human resources

_____

b) interdependence

_____

c) workforce

_____

d) population

_____

e) employment

_____

f) unemployment

_____

g) underemployment

_____

2 Examine the images below and for each image state whether the activity shown is a primary, secondary, tertiary or quaternary industrial activity. Give reasons for your answers. A page reference from the *Social Studies Atlas for Jamaica* is also provided for each image. Read the pages to help you with this exercise.

a)   Page 37

b)   Page 37

c)   Page 38

d) Page 38

e) Page 41

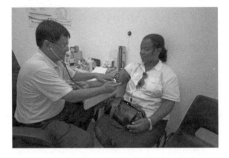

f) Page 44

g) Page 44

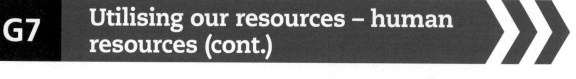
3 Examine page 41 of the *Social Studies Atlas for Jamaica*. At the top right hand corner of the page is information for the population structure of Jamaica. This information is presented using population pyramids. Let us study the population pyramids and learn more about them by completing the exercise below.

a) Complete the following sentences. Use the words provided in brackets at the end of each paragraph. Each word is to be used only once.

i) A population pyramid provides information about the
_____ of the population. The males are shown on the
_____ side, while the _____ are on the
right side. **(left, gender, females)**

ii) The numbers on the left and right sides of the pyramids are age
_____. Each group increases by _____
years. Therefore, at the _____ of the pyramid
ages _____ to four, are followed by ages five
to _____ directly above. The groups continue
_____ like this. **(upwards, groups, nine, zero, five, bottom)**

iii) The numbers at the bottom of the pyramids are _____.
These numbers must be read from the _____ of
the pyramid at the bottom. We must start where the number
zero is between the _____ and pink columns. Each
full _____ represents 1% of the total population.
(percentages, blue, middle, square)

iv) Therefore, to calculate a percentage of _____ we start
at the bottom middle zero and _____ the blue squares
going left. To calculate a percentage of females, we start at the same
zero, but this time we count the _____ squares going
right. **(pink, males, count)**

b) Answer each of the following questions using the two population pyramids.

i) Which two years are represented in the population pyramids?

_____

ii) Which age groups do you think would be retired people?

_____

iii) Which age groups do you think would be school age children?

_____

iv) Which age groups do you think would be a part of the workforce?

_____

v) Complete the table below by estimating the percentages in each category. Remember that one square represents 1%. Circle the correct answer from the set of choices provided.

Year	Gender	Age Group	Percentage
1957	Males ONLY	0–14	20% 8% 2%
1957	Females ONLY	0–14	4% 40% 19%
1957	Males and Females	15–59	54% 26% 6%
1957	Males ONLY	60–64	30% 1% 10%

Year	Gender	Age Group	Percentage
2017	Males ONLY	0–14	20% 12% 42%
2017	Females ONLY	0–14	11% 38% 80%
2017	Males and Females	15–59	32% 14% 64%
2017	Females ONLY	70–79	2% 22% 37%

c) The workforce is the part of the population which creates income for a country. They support children and retired people directly by working as family units, and indirectly by paying taxes which help the government to keep the country running. Circle true or false for each statement below.

i) A population pyramid with a very wide top has a low number of retired people.

true   false

ii) A large workforce is good for a country.

true   false

iii) A population pyramid with a very wide middle and a narrow top and a narrow bottom has a large workforce.

true   false

iv) A high number of school age children in a population right now is likely to result in a large workforce in the same population in the future.

true   false

v) If a country's workforce is large but unemployment is high, citizens may turn to crime to meet their needs.

true   false

vi) A country with a large workforce and very few children will eventually have a large retired population and a small workforce.

true   false

4 **Read pages 20–21 in the *Social Studies Atlas for Jamaica* to answer the following questions about the movement of human resources in the Caribbean.**

a) What caused the first large movement of people into the Caribbean for labour and where did these workers come from?

_____

b) When was the next large movement of people into the Caribbean for labour and where did these workers come from?

_____

_____

c) What is the main difference between the labour movements in 1500–1870 and the 1830s–1920s?

_____

d) Why did Caribbean workers migrate to Britain between 1945 and 1962?

_____

_____

e) List two reasons why many Caribbean workers migrated to Latin America from the 1850s to the 1930s?

_____

_____

5 **Extended Learning: carry out some research on the internet to complete the following assignments.**

a) Look at the image of 'coral reef damage' on page 23 of the *Social Studies Atlas for Jamaica*. Use this image as the centrepiece for a flyer that educates dive tour operators about coral bleaching. Your flyer should also include rules tourists can follow while diving that will protect coral.

b) Look at the image at the bottom right of page 71 of the *Social Studies Atlas for Jamaica*. Use this photo as the centrepiece for a letter to a mining company's executives, educating them about the negative impacts of mining on the environment. Your letter should include information about afforestation and how the company can support afforestation.

Grade 7 – Term 2, Unit 3

In this unit you will learn about how society is organised in **social groups and institutions**.

Humans are highly social and are naturally drawn to each other. Societies are therefore organised into **social groups** with varying closeness, purpose and permanence. The interaction of these social groups is the foundation of many of our **institutions**.

1 Use your *Collins Jamaican School Dictionary* and other sources to match the terms from the box to the correct definitions.

institution	social groups	group cohesion
pressure group	deviance	values
folkways	mores	taboo
socialisation	social control	norm

a) A social custom that some words, subjects or actions must be avoided because they are considered, embarrassing or offensive.

_____

b) The bonds, forces or factors among people working in a group that push them closer together.

_____

c) Behaviour that is unacceptable or different from that considered as normal.

_____

d) Methods of making a society work in a particular way using a set of rules and standards for individual behaviour.

_____

e) The moral principles and beliefs a group or a person thinks are important.

_____

f) A usual or expected thing.

_____

g) A group of people who try hard to persuade society to do something for a particular cause.

_____

h) A custom or system regarded as an important tradition within society.

_____

i) Learning to behave in a way that is acceptable to society.

_____

j) A set of people linked together in society or life.

_____

k) The essential or characteristic customs and conventions of a community.

_____

l) The traditional behaviour or way of life of a particular community or group of people.

_____

2 Locate and examine the following images from the _Social Studies Atlas for Jamaica_ which show different groups. Two of the images depict a social group and two do not.

a) Examine each image then complete the table below.

Image	Is this a social group? YES/NO	Explain why this is a social group or not	If this is a social group, what type of group is it?
Ginger peelers, page 28			
Downtown, Kingston, page 31			
Crop Over, Barbados, page 61			
Steelband, Trinidad, page 67			

b) For the two images depicting social groups, explain the importance of the group to society.

_____

_____

_____

_____

_____

_____

3 Extended Learning: examine the images on page 15 of the *Social Studies Atlas for Jamaica*. Carry out some research to write a case study on the Red Cross.

a) Begin with a few basic facts about the Red Cross.

b) The Red Cross is a secondary and formal social group, explain why.

c) Describe the functions of the Red Cross.

d) Explain the importance of the Red Cross in society.

e) Identify one local group, one regional group and one international group similar to the Red Cross.

Grade 7 – Term 2, Unit 4

In this unit you will learn about **the family**, types of families and how they are organised and roles of family members.

The **family** is the most important social unit. It is in families that most individuals are socialised to the expectations, values and norms of the society in which they live. However, each family is different since the members bring their own unique history and background and experience to the group and the **family structures** can vary as well. A functioning family should meet certain needs of the members that fall into three broad categories: physical/economic support, socialisation, emotional support.

1 Use the *Collins Jamaican School Dictionary* and other sources to complete the concept map below by filling in the definitions of the terms in each box.

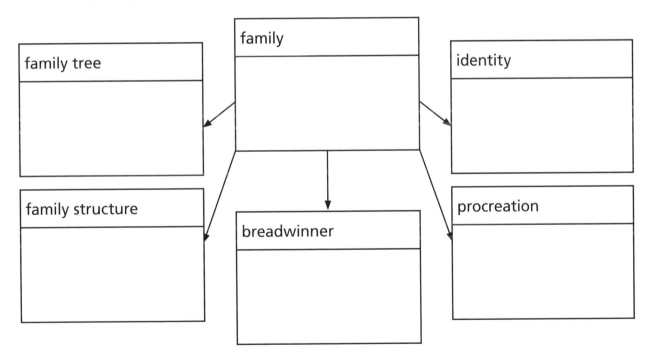

2 Examine the following images in the *Social Studies Atlas for Jamaica*, to write short sentences on some of the different functions of the family.

a)   Page 41, Doctor in Montego Bay

_____

b)   Page 37, Fishing in Portland Bight

_____

c)   Page 50, Street sellers in Haiti

_____

3 Study the population growth graph on page 41 of the *Social Studies Atlas for Jamaica*.

a)   Describe how the population has changed from 1960 to 2016?

_____

b)   Explain which function of the family was important to this change.

_____

c)   Compare the population pyramids from 1957 and 2017 on page 41 of the *Social Studies Atlas for Jamaica*. In which year was the percentage of children in the population higher?

_____

d)   Suggest a reason for your observation in question 2c.

_____

4 Examine the bauxite and alumina production graph on page 38 of the *Social Studies Atlas for Jamaica* to learn about the changes that have occurred in this industry.

a)   State two years in which production was high and two years in which it was low.

_____

b) Briefly explain how these changes in the bauxite and alumina industries could have affected families and prevented them from carrying out their functions effectively.

_____

_____

5 Examine the net migration graph for 2002–2013 on page 41 of the _Social Studies Atlas for Jamaica_. Net migration is the difference between the number of people entering and leaving a country. If net migration is positive it means more people enter than those who leave. If net migration is negative it means more people are leaving.

a) What type of net migration did Jamaica experience between 2002 and 2013? Circle your response below.

Positive net migration   Negative net migration

b) In which year was the net migration

i) highest?   _____   **ii)** lowest?   _____

c) Give some reasons why a family or family members may migrate out of a country.

_____

_____

_____

_____

d) Outline the challenges a family may face when one or both parents migrate out of the country.

_____

_____

_____

_____

6 Extended Learning: work in groups to research each of the following family types: nuclear family, extended family, single-parent family, grandparent family, childless family. Create a poster describing the family types and listing some disadvantages and advantages of each family type.

Grade 7 – Term 3, Unit 1

In this unit you will learn about how the movements of the Earth through space affect life on Earth.

As the Earth revolves around the Sun and rotates on its axis, different parts of the planet either point towards the Sun or away from it. This influences how much sunlight different parts of the Earth receive. Additionally, the length of time that each place receives sunlight also changes. This creates the seasons and influences the length of day and night across the globe.

1 Use the *Collins Jamaican School Dictionary* and other sources to define the following terms.

a) rotation

b) revolution

c) longitude

d) hemisphere

e) time zone

f) International Date Line

g) Greenwich Meridian

h) Greenwich Mean Time

_____

i) seasons

_____

j) axis

_____

k) tides

_____

2 Use pages 92 and 93 of the *Social Studies Atlas for Jamaica* to label the following diagram to show:

a) The Equator

b) The Tropic of Cancer

c) The Tropic of Capricorn

d) The North Pole

e) The South Pole

f) Northern Hemisphere

g) Southern Hemisphere

h) The following lines of latitude: 20°N, 40°N, 60°N, 80°N, 20°S, 40°S, 60°S, 80°S.

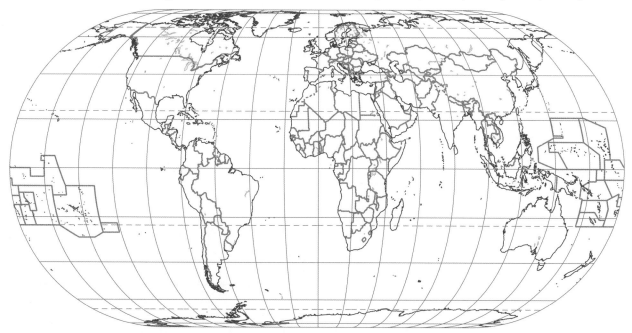

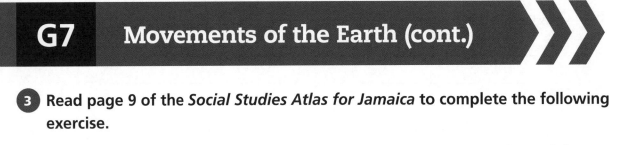

3 **Read page 9 of the *Social Studies Atlas for Jamaica* to complete the following exercise.**

a)   Explain with the aid of a diagram how rotation creates night and day.

_____

_____

_____

_____

_____

_____

_____

_____

_____

_____

b)   Explain with the aid of a diagram how revolution causes the seasons.

_____

_____

_____

_____

_____

_____

_____

_____

_____

4 Use other resources to help you understand how people's activities may change with the seasons. Share what you find in a short summary below.

_____

_____

_____

_____

_____

_____

5 Read page 7 of the *Social Studies Atlas for Jamaica* on Time zones. Use the time zone map at the bottom of page 7 and the political map on pages 92 and 93 to complete the following exercise.

Greenwich Mean Time	Capital city	City time
8:00 a.m.	Kingston	
9:00 a.m.	Moscow	
3:45 a.m.	Mogadishu	
1:20 a.m.	Riyadh	
12:00 a.m. (noon)	Brasilia	
5:00 p.m.	Tokyo	
12:00 p.m. (midnight)	Cape Town	
9:15 p.m.	Washington D.C.	
2:30 p.m.	Kathmandu	

6 Read page 7 of the *Social Studies Atlas for Jamaica* on Time zones. Use the time zone map at the bottom of page 7 and the physical map on pages 94 and 95 to complete the following exercise.

Greenwich Mean Time	Landform	Time at Landform
1:30 a.m.	Mt Everest	
11:00 a.m.	East China Sea	
5:30 a.m.	Hudson Bay	
9:30 a.m.	Panama Canal	
12:00 a.m. (noon)	Mt Kenya	
7:45 p.m.	Milwaukee Deep	
12:00 p.m. (midnight)	Aoraki/Mt Cook	
10:00 p.m.	Caspian Sea	
3:30 p.m.	Denali/Mt McKinley	

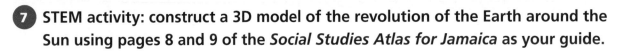

7 STEM activity: construct a 3D model of the revolution of the Earth around the Sun using pages 8 and 9 of the *Social Studies Atlas for Jamaica* as your guide.

Your model must clearly show:

– the Sun larger than the Earth

– the Earth tilted on its axis, the north and south poles, the tropics and the Equator

– the Earth in the four different positions at the start of each season (you may want to create a static model with the Earth shown at each of the four points shown in the *Social Studies Atlas for Jamaica* or you may create a moving model with a single Earth that can move around the Sun)

– the correct direction of rotation and revolution of the Earth.

Use your creativity and check online for ways to create a moving model or to get the Sun to light up. Remember – always ask an adult for help when doing online research and when constructing your model.

Grade 7 – Term 3, Unit 2

In this unit you will learn about interdependence and why it is an important theme in the Caribbean.

The Caribbean is a small region, and the countries that are a part of it are even smaller. This means that working together and sharing resources and ideas is important for reaching larger goals that each country may not be able to reach on its own. The Caribbean has experienced attempts at integration from colonial times until now as a useful method of creating power on the world stage.

1 Use the *Collins Jamaican School Dictionary* and other sources to define the following terms.

a) integration

_____

b) cooperation

_____

c) regional

_____

d) bilateral

_____

e) multilateral

_____

f) independent

_____

g) interdependent

_____

h) regional agreement

_____

i) bilateral agreement

_____

j) multilateral agreement

_____

2 Examine page 39 of the *Social Studies Atlas for Jamaica* to complete the following exercise.

a) From which country did Jamaica make its largest purchase of imports?

_____

b) From which two countries did Jamaica purchase the same percentage of imports?

_____

c) What percentage of exported Jamaican goods went to Canada?

_____

d) Which European country received the largest percentage of Jamaican exports?

_____

e) What percentage of Jamaican imports were food products?

_____

f) List the types of products which each made up 5% of Jamaican imports?

_____

g) What percentage of Jamaican exports were vegetables and animals?

_____

h) What type of product did Jamaica export the largest percentage of in 2016?

_____

i) Look back at the meaning of the term *interdependent* then briefly explain how these graphs help to show interdependence.

_____

_____

3 **Examine page 39 and the political map on pages 92 and 93 of the _Social Studies Atlas for Jamaica_ to complete the map below.**

a) Shade and label each of Jamaica's named export and import partners. Each partner should be shaded a different colour.

b) Add lines joining each country to Jamaica and show the direction of trade by adding arrows. Use blue lines to show imports and green lines to show exports.

c) Add the percentage to each corresponding trade line.

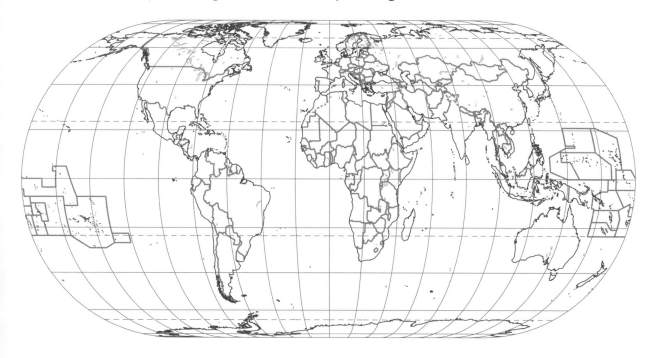

4 **Extended Learning: Case Study: Examine the image of water pollution on page 36 of the *Social Studies Atlas for Jamaica* and do some research to answer the questions below.**

a) Identify the area where this problem exists on the map of Jamaica below and identify communities nearby which may be negatively affected. Your map must be complete with a key and a compass rose.

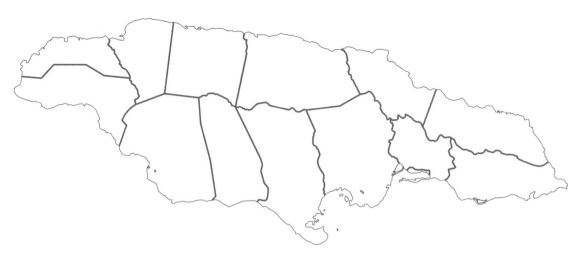

b) Describe the problem as shown in the image and outline its possible causes and impacts.

_____

_____

_____

_____

_____

_____

_____

_____

c) Come up with an action plan for the members of the community to solve the problem. Use the template below to outline two actions you would take.

ACTION PLAN

Action	Describe the action in detail and steps you would take	List different resources you would need to carry out the action	List key people who would play a role in the action (for example, Councillor or MP, Citizens Association)	Time frame, how long would it take to complete this action?
1.				
2.				

5 **Examine page 45 of the *Social Studies Atlas for Jamaica*.**

a) List the countries which are members of each of the following regional organisations.

i) CARICOM

_____

ii) CARIFTA

_____

iii) OECS

_____

b) Name the regional organisation that has the largest membership.

_____

c) What are the main functions of this organisation?

_____

d) Name the two countries that are members of this organisation but their main language is not English.

_____

e) Complete the map below by shading and labelling the countries that are members of this organisation.

f) What are two advantages of regional integration?

_____

_____

_____

_____

g) What are two disadvantages of regional integration?

_____

_____

_____

_____

Grade 7 – Term 3, Unit 3

In this unit you will learn about the importance of protecting our environment.

The Caribbean is a particularly delicate ecological site because the multitude of islands allow for many unique habitats where plants and animals can adapt and evolve into a high number of endemic species. Unfortunately, the small size of the islands and limited resource access often mean that these plants and animals are harmed as humans use resources. Conservation efforts are therefore very important in the Caribbean.

1 Use the *Collins Jamaican School Dictionary* and other sources to define the following terms.

a) sustainable practices

_____

b) conservation

_____

c) preservation

_____

d) reuse

_____

e) recycle

_____

f) reduce

_____

g) protected area

_____

h) endangered species

_____

i) endemic species

_____

j) biodiversity

_____

k) energy conservation

_____

l) energy efficient

_____

2 **Read the text about endangered species in Jamaica on page 36 of the _Social Studies Atlas for Jamaica_ and respond to the questions below.**

a) What percentage of Jamaica's bird and animal species are endemic to the island? _____

b) Create a bar graph to show the number of different species that are now endangered.

3 Extended Learning: create a poster identifying three endemic Jamaican animals that are also endangered. Your poster should include a picture of each species and information on:

a) where they are found

b) why they are endangered

c) what is being done to protect them.

4 Extended Learning: Case study: Blue and John Crow Mountains National Park

a) Identify the location of Blue and John Crow Mountains National park on the map below. Shade and label the area. Your map should also include the parish names, three main rivers and the location of five important towns. It must be complete with a key and a compass rose.

b) Carry out some research to find out:

i) when this area was designated a protected area and other facts about the park

ii) why this area was designated a protected area

iii) what rules and regulations are in place to protect the park.

_____

_____

_____

_____

_____

_____

_____

_____

_____

_____

Grade 8 – Term 1, Unit 1

In this unit you will learn about Vision 2030, the National Development Plan for Jamaica.

Vision 2030 is a long-term plan for Jamaica's development based on nationalist interests. Vision 2030 considers Jamaica's unique culture and history, the needs of the present society, and outlines strategies that will help fulfil these needs. It encompasses social, economic, cultural and environmental points that will guide decision making and help to establish Jamaica as the place of choice within the Caribbean to live, work, raise families and do business.

1 a) Use the *Collins Jamaican School Dictionary* and other sources to complete the concept map below by filling in the definitions of the terms in each box.

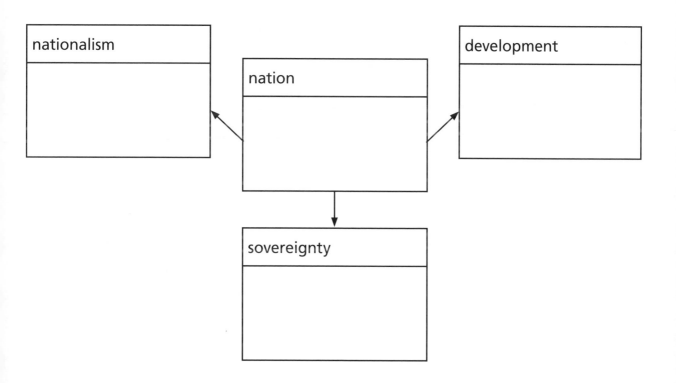

b) Use the terms in question 1a to complete each of the following sentences.

i) When a country's people progress from low-income households to middle and high-income households this is a sign of economic _____.

ii) The success of a _____ depends on its natural resources and its human resources.

iii) A good citizen has a strong feeling of _____.

iv) The ability of citizens to exercise their democratic rights in public elections is one way that a country practices its _____.

2 The national development strategy Vision 2030 is based on four national goals:

Goal 1: Jamaicans are empowered to achieve their fullest potential.

a) i) Define the word empower.

_____

ii) Define the word potential.

_____

iii) In your own words, explain what you think this goal means.

_____

_____

b) There are four National Outcomes used to measure the success of *Goal 1* of Vision 2030. State what you think each outcome means and why you think achieving it is a good way to empower Jamaicans.

Outcome 1: A Healthy and Stable Population

_____

_____

_____

_____

Outcome 3: Effective Social Protection

_____

_____

Outcome 4: Authentic and Transformational Culture

_____

_____

c)   Examine the images and health statistics on page 41 in the *Social Studies Atlas for Jamaica* to complete the following.

   i)   Which of the outcomes for *Goal 1* is the image reflective of? Explain.

   _____

   _____

   ii) Based on the health statistics we can assess *Goal 1*. In which areas is Jamaica doing well and in which areas is harder work needed to achieve the goal?

   _____

   _____

d)   Read Famous Jamaicans on page 43 of the *Social Studies Atlas for Jamaica* and use the *Collins Jamaican School Dictionary* to answer the following questions on *Goal 1* of Vision 2030.

   i)   List three famous Jamaicans who were empowered in sports.

   _____

   ii) List three famous Jamaicans who were empowered in music.

   _____

iii) List three famous Jamaicans who were empowered in the arts.

_____

iv) Describe how the success of these famous Jamaicans has benefited Jamaica.

_____

v) List three more areas in which Jamaicans should be empowered.

_____

vi) Explain why empowerment in a variety of areas is important.

_____

Goal 2: The Jamaican society is secure, cohesive and just.

e) Use the _Collins Jamaican School Dictionary_ to assist with the following questions on _Goal 2_ of Vision 2030.

i) Define the word secure.

_____

ii) Define the word cohesive.

_____

iii) Define the word just.

_____

iv) In your own words, explain what you think this goal means.

_____

_____

v) Why do you think it is important for Jamaica to be secure, cohesive and just?

_____

_____

vi) List two things you can do every day to make Jamaica more secure, cohesive and just.

_____

_____

_____

_____

f) Read National Heroes on page 43 of the *Social Studies Atlas for Jamaica* then complete the following.

i) For each National Hero, describe how their actions helped make their society more secure, cohesive and just.

Paul Bogle

_____

_____

Sir Alexander Bustamante

_____

_____

Marcus Garvey

_____

_____

George William Gordon

_____

_____

Norman Manley

_____

_____

Queen Nanny

_____

_____

Samuel Sharpe

_____

_____

ii) Examine the Government structure chart on page 24 of the _Social Studies Atlas for Jamaica_. For each of the three main branches of government, describe one way you think the government can make Jamaica more secure, cohesive and just.

Legislature

_____

_____

Executive

_____

_____

Judiciary

_____

_____

iii) State whether you think this goal can still be achieved if one of the branches of government is removed or is no longer working effectively. Explain your answer.

_____

_____

Goal 3: Jamaica's economy is prosperous.

G8

g) Use the *Collins Jamaican School Dictionary* and other sources to answer the following questions.

   i) Define the word economy.

   _____

   ii) Define the word prosperous.

   _____

   iii) In your own words, explain what you think this goal means.

   _____

   _____

   iv) Explain why you think a prosperous economy is important for Jamaica's development.

   _____

   _____

   v) Define the word import.

   _____

   vi) Define the word export.

   _____

   vii) Define balance of trade.

   _____

   viii) Define positive balance of trade.

   _____

   ix) Define negative balance of trade.

   _____

x) Explain why exports are a good way to measure the prosperity of Jamaica's economy.

_____

_____

xi) Examine the balance of trade graph on page 39 of the *Social Studies Atlas for Jamaica*. Has Jamaica's balance of trade between 2005 and 2016 been positive or negative? Explain your answer.

_____

_____

xii) What impact do you think this pattern of trade has had on the Jamaican economy?

_____

_____

h) Examine page 39 of the *Social Studies Atlas for Jamaica* to select the correct answer from the options provided.

i) In which year from 2009 to 2016 was alumina export the highest?

2009   2015   2011

ii) How did bauxite export change from 2009 to 2016?

increased   decreased   stayed the same

iii) Between which two years from 2009 to 2016 did alumina export increase the most?

2009–2010   2010–2011   2015–2016

iv) In which year was chemical export higher than US$200 million?

2016   2012   2010

v) In which year was mineral fuel export the lowest?

2016   2010   2013

vi) In which year was sugar export less than rum export ONLY?

2015   2010   2012

vii) In which year was sugar export less than both rum and coffee exports?

2015   2010   2012

viii) What was the general trend in agriculture exports from 2009 to 2016?

increase   decrease   stayed the same

Goal 4: Jamaica has a healthy natural environment.

i) One outcome of this goal is to reduce our risk to hazards such as hurricanes. Read page 35 of the *Social Studies Atlas for Jamaica* to complete the following exercise.

  i) Explain why Jamaica is regularly hit by hurricanes.

  _____

  _____

  ii) What are the two major issues the island is vulnerable to due to hurricanes?

  _____

  iii) What was the total damage caused by hurricanes Dennis (2005), Gustav (2008) and Sandy (2012)?

  _____

  iv) What is the likely impact on our development if we do not find ways to reduce our risk to hazards such as hurricanes?

  _____

  _____

j) Another outcome of this goal is the sustainable management of the environment and resources. Read page 36 of the *Social Studies Atlas for Jamaica* to complete the following exercise.

  i) For each environmental issue below, state one way it is caused and one solution to the problem.

Deforestation

_____

_____

_____

_____

Mining damage

_____

_____

_____

_____

Water pollution

_____

_____

_____

_____

Endangered species

_____

_____

_____

_____

ii) Explain why you think a healthy natural environment is important to Jamaica's development.

_____

_____

k) Extended Learning:

i) Conduct a survey among five adults and five students to find out what they know about Vision 2030. Record your findings using a table like the one below.

	Number of persons		
	Very knowledgeable	Somewhat knowledgeable	No knowledge
Adults			
Students			
Total			

ii) Carry out some research to find three methods to increase public awareness of the National Goals of the national development strategy Vision 2030. Describe:

one way to increase awareness at home among your family members

_____

_____

_____

_____

one way to increase awareness at your school among the students and teachers

_____

_____

_____

_____

one way to increase awareness in your neighbourhood

_____

_____

_____

_____

Grade 8 – Term 1, Unit 2

In this unit you will learn why communication is important, learn about its various forms and explore the influence of media on everyday life.

Communication is a characteristic of human society that separates humans from animals. The ability to understand meaning through language, symbols and actions is key to how we experience the world around us. This has produced a wide range of applications in the form of media which affect our decision making.

1 **a)** Use the *Collins Jamaican School Dictionary* and other sources to complete the concept map below by filling in the definitions of the terms in each box.

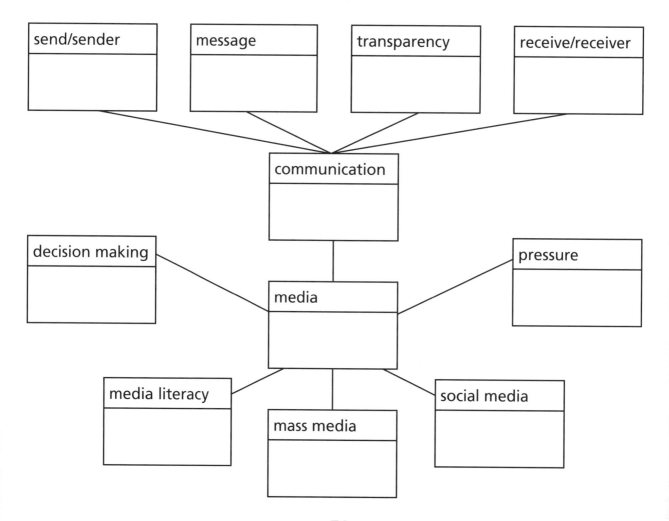

b) Use the terms in the box provided to complete each of the following sentences.

sender	receiver	message
transparency	communication	mass media
media literacy	decision making	social media
pressure group		

i) _____ is important in a business if employees are to be satisfied with decisions made by management.

ii) The information that citizens have about an issue can affect their _____ in a democratic society.

iii) The _____ of an email must know the email address of the person they are contacting.

iv) The ability to verify the source of a message is an important _____ skill.

v) A teacher may ask a student to take a _____ to another student.

vi) Facebook is a large _____ company.

vii) One of the oldest forms of electronic _____ is radio broadcasting.

viii) When you accept a letter from the postman you become the _____ of the letter.

ix) Interpersonal _____ occurs when the sender and receiver of the message are face to face.

x) Another name for a _____ is a lobby or advocacy group.

2 Match each form of communication on the left with the correct example on the right. Each set is grouped in opposite pairs.

nonverbal   saying 'Good morning' to your classmate
verbal   waving at a passer-by

formal   email of a cover letter for a job application
informal   sending a funny story to your friend on WhatsApp

written   a large red cross on the side of a hospital building
visual   a letter from your parent to the teacher

3 Examine the image of the Red Cross in Haiti and data on recent hurricanes on page 15 of the *Social Studies Atlas for Jamaica* to complete the exercise.

a) Describe two ways you think the media could be used by organisations like the Red Cross after a natural disaster.

_____

_____

_____

_____

b) i) What was the highest number of deaths caused by recent hurricanes? Record the year, country and the name of the hurricane.

_____

ii) Explain how newspapers and radio broadcasting could be used during hurricane season to encourage hurricane preparedness and public safety.

_____

_____

c) The use of social media is very popular today.

i) Describe how social media could be used immediately after a hurricane to benefit the public.

_____

_____

ii) State one way in which social media could be used in a negative way during times of disaster.

_____

_____

d) Explain why it might be difficult to use electronic media effectively after a hurricane.

_____

_____

4 **Examine the tourism graphs at the bottom of page 44 of the _Social Studies Atlas for Jamaica_ to complete the exercise.**

a) **i)** Describe the general trend in stop-over visitor arrivals 2001–2016.

_____

ii) How do you think increased use of social media from 2001 to 2016 may have influenced this trend?

_____

_____

b) **i)** In which three months in 2016 were stop-over visitor arrivals highest?

_____

ii) Suggest how mass media could be used during the remaining months to increase stop-over visitor arrivals.

_____

_____

c) **i)** In which years from 2001 to 2016 were cruise passenger arrivals less than 1 000 000?

_____

ii) Describe how mass media could be used to increase cruise passenger arrivals.

_____

_____

d) **i)** From which country was the largest percentage of stop-over visitor arrivals in 2016?

_____

ii) What percentage of stop-over visitor arrivals in 2016 came for the purpose of visiting friends and relatives?

_____

iii) Describe how mass media could be used to increase stop-over visitor arrivals from Canada for the purpose of business.

_____

_____

5 Examine the image of Dunn's River Falls on page 31 of the *Social Studies Atlas for Jamaica* and the image of Bob Marley on page 43 of the *Social Studies Atlas for Jamaica*. Points of interest such as Dunn's River Falls or events such as concerts performed by musicians are examples of *social activities*. Social activities are an important part of *social life* as people spend time doing enjoyable things with each other to create connections and relationships.

a) For two other points of interest in Jamaica find a picture, from a magazine or printed from an online source, and stick them into the boxes provided. Label each box with the name of the location.

b) For two famous Jamaican musicians, find a picture from a magazine or printed from an online source and stick them in the boxes provided. Label each box with the name of the musician.

c) Describe one way that you would use social media to plan a social activity at one of the points of interest in question 5a.

_____

_____

d) Suggest how the media can affect how people make decisions about which points of interest to go to or events to attend for social activity.

_____

_____

e) Describe how people can use the information online/on the internet to plan their social life.

_____

_____

6 **Examine the Government structure chart at the bottom of page 24 of the _Social Studies Atlas for Jamaica_.**

a) State which part of the government is made up of members elected by public vote.

_____

b) State the main function of these persons or this arm of the government.

_____

c) Describe how each of the following types of mass media could be used to influence how people vote during an election:

i) print media

_____

_____

ii) radio broadcasts

_____

_____

iii) television broadcasting

_____

_____

iv) social media

_____

_____

7 **Access to information is very important and the media plays a key role in informing the public.**

a) Explain two ways in which people's attitude and behaviour could be changed if the information on AIDS/HIV on page 41 of the *Social Studies Atlas for Jamaica* were shared by the media.

_____

_____

_____

_____

b) Which form of media do you think would be most effective in sharing this information? Explain your answer.

_____

_____

Grade 8 – Term 1, Unit 3

In this unit you will learn about cultural icons and why they are significant in Jamaican culture.

A **cultural icon** is a symbol, logo, picture, name, face, person, building or other image used to represent the culture or an aspect of culture in a society. It is easily recognised and generally represents an object or idea with great cultural significance to a wide cultural group. It has a special status as representing, or being important to or loved by, a particular group of people, a place, or a period in history.

1 Use the *Collins Jamaican School Dictionary* and other sources to complete the concept map below by filling in the definitions of the terms in each box.

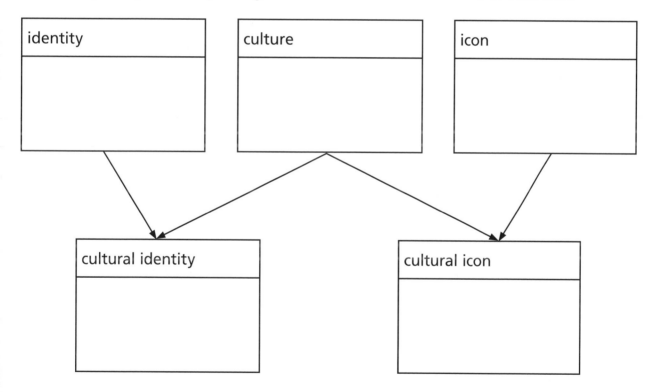

identity

culture

icon

cultural identity

cultural icon

2 The following exercise will help you to learn more about the concept of the Jamaican cultural icon.

a) Preparatory reading and research: first, review pages 43 and 24 of the *Social Studies Atlas for Jamaica* to learn about some people and symbols that are Jamaican cultural icons. Check online sources such as the *Jamaica Information Service* and the *National Library of Jamaica* as well to learn even more about Jamaican cultural heritage and important cultural icons.

b) Use the information from your reading, the *Collins Jamaican School Dictionary* and other sources to help you complete this exercise.

  i) Cultural icons must satisfy certain criteria to be considered cultural icons. Define the word criterion/criteria.

  _____

  ii) Do you think that icons should meet criteria or should they simply be selected and acknowledged without using any criteria? Explain your answer.

  _____

  _____

  _____

c) Each word below is a criterion used to select cultural icons. For each word:

  i) Write a definition.

  ii) Unscramble the words in brackets to complete the sentence which describes the criterion.

  iii) Explain why you think each criterion is important for a cultural icon to meet.

  Recognisable

  i) Definition:

  _____

ii) A cultural icon should be recognisable. This means it is
_____ (elysia) identified so that it is quickly
_____ (inledk) with Jamaica by those who see it.

iii) Explain why it is important that a cultural icon be recognisable.

_____

_____

Representative

i) Definition:

_____

ii) A cultural icon should be representative. This means it is
_____ (drealet) to a larger _____ (adie)
or concept about Jamican culture.

iii) Explain why it is important that a cultural icon be representative.

_____

_____

Significant

i) Definition:

_____

ii) A cultural icon should be significant. This means it _____
(triconbuets) in a major way to the _____ (arpt) of
culture it represents.

iii) Explain why it is important that a cultural icon be significant.

_____

_____

Unique

i) Definition:

_____

ii) A cultural icon should be unique. This means it is _____ (ditsctin) and special and cannot be _____ (fusecodn) with another culture or meaning.

iii) Explain why it is important that a cultural icon be unique.

_____

_____

Specific

i) Definition:

_____

ii) A cultural icon should be specific. This means the part of Jamaican culture it represents should be a _____ (parcutilar) time in history, _____ (caloiont), or group.

iii) Explain why it is important that a cultural icon be specific.

_____

_____

Beloved

i) Definition:

_____

ii) A cultural icon should be beloved. This means people should _____ (apciteapre) and embrace the icon as _____ (cisoupre).

iii) Explain why it is important that a cultural icon be beloved.

_____

_____

3 Five Jamaican cultural icons are listed in the box. Locate their birthplace on the map below and complete the appropriate box with information about their work or significance as a cultural icon. You may use information from the *Social Studies Atlas for Jamaica* and other sources to fill in the boxes.

Louise Bennett-Coverly	Ralston Milton 'Rex' Nettleford	
Veronica Campbell-Brown	Bob Marley	Barrington 'Barry' Watson

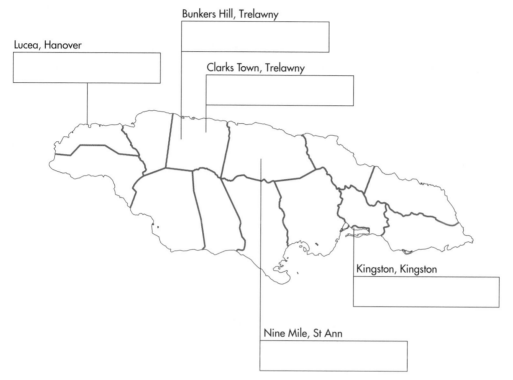

Bunkers Hill, Trelawny

Lucea, Hanover

Clarks Town, Trelawny

Kingston, Kingston

Nine Mile, St Ann

4 In Grade 7, Term 1, Unit 3 we noted that culture can be material or non-material, and classified some cultural images as material or non-material. Complete the following exercise to review these concepts.

a) Define material culture.

_____

b) The Tainos and Maroons left behind artefacts that were part of their material culture. Use the maps on page 42 of the *Social Studies Atlas for Jamaica* to complete the following questions.

i) Name two locations (parishes) where examples of Taino artefacts can possibly be found in Jamaica.

_____

_____

ii) Name two locations where examples of Maroon artefacts can be found in Jamaica.

_____

_____

c) Jamaica's colonial history left behind material culture in the form of architecture that reflects the influence of Spanish and English culture in Jamaica.

i) Using the Spanish Settlement map on page 42 of the *Social Studies Atlas for Jamaica*, name two locations (place names and parishes) where Spanish colonial architecture would have once existed in Jamaica.

_____

_____

ii) English colonial architecture can still be found across the island. Two examples of this are shown on page 33 of the *Social Studies Atlas for Jamaica*. List their locations and find out when they were built.

_____

_____

d) Modern-day Jamaican culture is made up of material things that are important to Jamaicans and that non-Jamaicans can easily associate with Jamaican culture. Use page 24 of the *Social Studies Atlas for Jamaica* to complete this exercise.

i) Colour the Jamaican flag and describe what each colour represents.

_____

_____

_____

_____

_____

ii) Colour the Jamaican national fruit, the ackee, below and briefly describe how it is prepared.

_____

_____

_____

_____

_____

_____

iii) For each important cultural location listed below find a photo or image from a magazine or online and paste it next to the parish where it is found. Describe why each location is important to Jamaican culture.

Blue Lagoon, Port Antonio	Montego Bay Cruise Port
Downtown, Kingston	Nassau Mountains
UWI, Mona Campus	

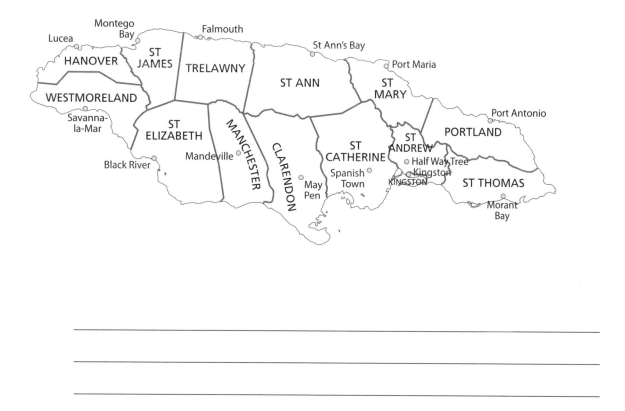

_____

_____

_____

_____

_____

_____

_____

_____

_____

e) Define non-material culture.

_____

f) Identify elements of non-material culture that would be represented by some of the famous Jamaicans mentioned on page 43 of the *Social Studies Atlas for Jamaica*.

_____

_____

g) A proverb is a saying in general use, stating a general truth or piece of advice. Proverbs are an important part of non-material culture. Write three Jamaican proverbs and explain their meaning.

Proverb 1

_____

_____

_____

_____

Proverb 2

_____

_____

_____

_____

_____

_____

_____

_____

h) A custom is a habitual way of doing something. Customs are important to non-material culture. Describe:

i) a Jamaican custom your family practises

_____

_____

_____

ii) a Jamaican custom your school practises

_____

_____

_____

iii) a Jamaican custom your neighbourhood practises

_____

_____

_____

5 Historic events often influence culture. Examine the timeline on page 42 of the *Social Studies Atlas for Jamaica*. Select five historic events which influenced Jamaican culture and create your own timeline to show them.

Grade 8 – Term 2, Unit 1

In this unit you will learn about the diversity of the Caribbean landscape, how it influences the activities we engage in and how we in turn influence the various landscapes.

In the Caribbean, many factors have produced a variety of **landscapes**. One of the most influential of these is **geology**. In order to make the best use of land resources with respect to human activity we must understand how differences in geology create the landscapes we live on and what we need to do to ensure we practise sustainable human activities that meet our needs but also protect the landscape.

1 Use the *Collins Jamaican School Dictionary* and other sources to define the following terms.

a) rock

_____

b) soil

_____

c) topography

_____

d) bauxite

_____

e) karst landscape

_____

f) limestone

_____

g) volcanic

_____

h) settlement

_____

i) communication

_____

j) mining

_____

k) quarrying

_____

2 **Examine pages 16 and 17 of the _Social Studies Atlas for Jamaica_ and other sources to complete the following exercise.**

a) Match the rock type on the left with the correct description on the right.

igneous   Formed when the minerals in one rock type are transformed by heat and pressure to form different rocks.

metamorphic   Formed when bits and pieces of rocks, soil and other small particles build up together over time.

sedimentary   Formed when molten rocks (magma or lava) cool and become solid.

b) Group the rocks in the box into the correct circles by their types.

limestone	granite	quartzite	andesite	sandstone
shale	marble	basalt	gneiss	diamond
coal	rock salt	obsidian	pumice	schist

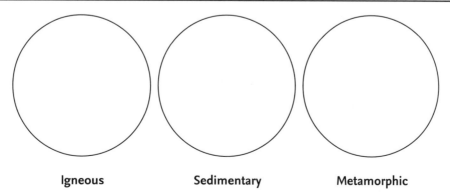

Igneous   Sedimentary   Metamorphic

c) Complete the map of the Caribbean below by using one colour to shade the volcanic islands and another to shade the limestone islands. Be sure to include a key on your complete map. Use page 17 of the *Social Studies Atlas for Jamaica* and other resources.

3 The landscape can influence where people live and also the types of activities they engage in.

a) Compare the physical map on pages 26–27 of the *Social Studies Atlas for Jamaica* with the urban centres map on page 40.

i) Identify the urban centres shown on the map on page 40. Use the maps on pages 26–31 to help name them.

_____

_____

ii) Describe the location of the majority of these urban centres and explain how the physical landscape helped to influence this pattern.

_____

_____

iii) Several sections on the Urban Centres map show no towns or urban centres. Compare with the Jamaica Physical map to identify two of these areas and why this may be so.

_____

_____

b) Compare the physical map on pages 26–27 of the *Social Studies Atlas for Jamaica* with the communications map on page 39.

i) On the map of Jamaica below: draw in the main roads and highways; shade and label the major mountains; insert a key and title for the map.

ii) Describe the distribution pattern of the main roads and highways.

_____

_____

_____

_____

iii) Explain how the physical landscape may have influenced this distribution.

_____

_____

_____

_____

4 Examine the images on pages 36 and 38 of the *Social Studies Atlas for Jamaica* and other sources for information and write a short essay on how human activities can influence the landscape. Your essay should include both negative and positive impacts.

_____

_____

_____

_____

_____

_____

_____

_____

_____

_____

_____

_____

_____

_____

_____

_____

_____

5 **a)** Examine the image of Dunn's River Falls, St Ann, on page 31 of the *Social Studies Atlas for Jamaica* and that of bamboo rafting on page 44. Describe how the landscape has influenced the human activities in these areas.

_____

_____

_____

_____

b) Examine the images of the Pitch Lake, Maracas Bay and Port of Spain, Trinidad on page 64 of the *Social Studies Atlas for Jamaica*. For each image describe the landscape and topography and explain how it has influenced the types of human activity in each area.

Pitch Lake

_____

_____

_____

_____

Maracas Bay

_____

_____

_____

_____

Port of Spain

_____

_____

_____

_____

Grade 8 – Term 2, Unit 2

In this unit you will learn about economic institutions and their role in Jamaican society.

Economic institutions are concerned with managing money and wealth. Individuals may be limited in their ability to manage money and wealth due to various legal and social issues that govern the use, transfer and investment of money. Therefore, economic institutions are designed to provide us with all the knowledge and tools necessary to make the best use of our economic resources. When individuals can manage their economics well, it helps the economy and society as a whole.

1 Use the *Collins Jamaican School Dictionary* and other sources to define the following terms.

a) economic institution

_____

b) credit

_____

c) insurance

_____

d) thrift

_____

e) bank

_____

f) building society

_____

g) credit union

_____

h) credit

_____

i) loan

_____

2 Use the internet and other resources to research and list three characteristics of each economic institution listed. Find at least two characteristics that will help to distinguish one from the other.

a) bank

_____

_____

_____

b) credit union

_____

_____

_____

c) building society

_____

_____

_____

3 Examine the image of Downtown, Kingston, on page 31 of the *Social Studies Atlas for Jamaica*. Economic institutions are usually a part of scenes like this all over the world. As consumers shop and business people offer services downtown, economic institutions also set up alongside them for easy access and the management of funds.

    i) Describe what is seen in the image.

_____

ii) Describe three roles that the bank or credit union play in the lives of consumers or shoppers seen in the image.

_____

_____

_____

_____

_____

_____

iii) Describe three functions that these economic institutions would carry out for the business operators in the image.

_____

_____

_____

_____

_____

_____

iv) Some business operators and consumers do not use the services offered by economic institutions. State one disadvantage of this practice for each.

_____

_____

_____

_____

4 **Extended Learning: carry out some research and write a case study on the Bank of Jamaica.**

a)   Begin with a few basic facts about the Bank of Jamaica.

b)   Describe the function of the Bank of Jamaica.

c)   Describe the services the Bank of Jamaica offers.

Grade 8 – Term 2, Unit 3

In this unit you will learn about consumerism and the influence of consumers on production.

The needs and wants of individuals and of society as a whole will change over time. This means that the demand for certain products will vary, as will the ability of producers to supply these products. It is important to recognise that the factors of **supply** and **demand, production** and **consumption** are all related and can influence how consumers and business operators alike will behave. This influence can be seen from the level of a local neighbourhood shop up to the level of big businesses operating across the globe.

1 Use the *Collins Jamaican School Dictionary* and other sources to define the following terms.

a) goods

_____

b) services

_____

c) consumer

_____

d) consumption

_____

e) consumerism

_____

f) needs

_____

g) wants

_____

h) budget

_____

i) income

_____

j) expenditure

_____

k) globalisation

_____

2 Examine each of the following images in the *Social Studies Atlas for Jamaica*.
For each image state whether a production activity/producer is being shown or
consumption/consumer activity is shown or both. Explain you answer.

a) Page 37, Coffee harvesting in the Blue Mountains

_____

_____

b) Page 37, Fishing in Portland Bight

_____

_____

c) Page 41, Doctor in Montego Bay

_____

_____

d) Page 44, Bamboo rafting on the Martha Brae River

_____

_____

e) Page 50, Street sellers in Haiti

_____

_____

3 Examine the graph of Bauxite and alumina production, 1974–2016 on page 38 of the *Social Studies Atlas for Jamaica*.

a) From 1980 to 1985 there was a general decline in bauxite production. How could this have affected consumer demand for bauxite in markets dependent on Jamaican bauxite? Explain your answer.

_____

_____

_____

b) From 2000 to 2006 there was an increase in bauxite production. How could this have affected consumer demand for bauxite in markets dependent on Jamaican bauxite? Explain your answer.

_____

_____

_____

c) From 2008 to 2009 there was a sharp decline in bauxite production. How could changes in consumer demand have caused this to occur?

_____

_____

_____

Grade 8 – Term 3, Unit 1

In this unit you will learn about the causes and effects of climate change and discuss possible solutions to this issue.

Climate change has been described as the greatest threat to humanity that we currently face. This is because a stable climate is important to almost every aspect of human life. Food and water security, global commerce, communication and social justice are all affected by climate; therefore, understanding climate change is very important. Recent and continuing extreme events have made it clear that we are in the middle of a significant shift in climatic conditions. Understanding what has caused this shift and the extent to which the changes will occur is therefore important if we are to find effective methods of adapting to and reducing the impacts of these changes.

1 Use the *Collins Jamaican School Dictionary*, pages 22, 23, 100 and 101 of the *Social Studies Atlas for Jamaica* and other sources to complete the exercise below.

a) Define the following terms.

i) climate change

_____

ii) carbon emission

_____

iii) carbon footprint

_____

iv) carbon credit

_____

v) global warming

_____

vi) greenhouse gas

_____

vii) coral bleaching

_____

viii) sea level rise

_____

ix) carbon dioxide

_____

x) deforestation

_____

xi) carbon sink

_____

b) Read pages 100–101 of the _Social Studies Atlas for Jamaica_ to identify different evidence used by scientists to confirm that the climate is changing. Complete each paragraph below with the correct terms provided in the box. The paragraphs are related to the evidence of climate change.

i) As climate changes the _____ are becoming warmer. This is noteworthy because seas heat up more slowly than _____. Therefore, for the seas to _____ enough heat to raise their _____ the amount of heat being stored around the _____ must be _____.

Earth	continents	absorb	temperature
significant	oceans		

ii) Ice sheets are also called continental _____.
_____ monitor the size of ice sheets since higher
temperatures melt ice. Therefore, the rate at which ice sheets thaw
or freeze _____ a change in climate. Additionally,
ice sheets also function to _____ sunlight back out
into space. Hence, as ice sheets shrink, more sunlight is absorbed
at the Earth's _____ and global temperatures can
_____ even more.

reflect	increase	indicates	glaciers
environmentalists		surface	

iii) The ocean is a natural _____ because it absorbs
carbon dioxide (CO_2) from the atmosphere. However, when CO_2
_____ in water it creates a chemical called carbonic
acid. This means that as more CO_2 is released into the atmosphere
by _____ activities the ocean becomes more
_____. This is harmful to _____ life since
the usual sea _____ are changing and these animals are
unable to adjust.

acidic	carbon sink	dissolves	marine
conditions	human		

c) **Extended learning:** work in groups to create a project based on research
to find out how climate change has resulted in ANY TWO of the following
extreme events in the past 20 years:

*   heatwaves
*   coastal flooding
*   hurricanes
*   extreme cold, blizzards and ice storms

For each extreme event you should carry out the following tasks.

i)   Explain how climate change has caused these events to become
extreme.

ii) Research a specific occurrence of the event. For this occurrence, record
when and where it happened.

iii) Describe the impact of the event on property, life and economy and describe the impact of the event on the natural environment (landscapes, habitats and wildlife). Also, compare the event to other occurrences.

iv) Describe ways that these events could be mitigated.

v) Use photos, graphs, charts and diagrams to present some of your information and make your project more engaging.

d) Use page 100 of the *Social Studies Atlas for Jamaica* to complete the following exercise.

i) Complete the diagram below and write a short paragraph in your own words describing the greenhouse effect. Do further research to help explain the relationship between the greenhouse effect and climate change.

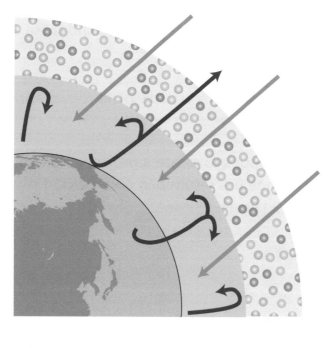

_____

_____

_____

_____

_____

ii) List two human activities that can increase the levels of the following greenhouse gases in the atmosphere.

carbon dioxide

_____

water vapour

_____

nitrous oxide

_____

methane

_____

e) Complete the following exercise using information from pages 22–23 of the _Social Studies Atlas for Jamaica_.

i) Describe the impact climate change has had on coral reefs in the Caribbean.

_____

_____

ii) What two effects of climate change have caused corals to be affected in this way?

_____

_____

iii) Name two Caribbean islands that experienced severe reef damage due to climate change.

_____

iv) List two Caribbean countries that have high levels of CO_2 emissions per person.

_____

v) What activity carried out in these two islands is responsible for these high emission levels?

_____

f) Complete the following exercise using information from the map on pages 100–101 of the *Social Studies Atlas for Jamaica*.

i) Change in ocean currents due to climate change have affected this ocean.

_____

ii) The Indian Ocean is experiencing what effect of climate change?

_____

iii) How many square kilometres (sq km) of Asia are affected by desertification?

_____

iv) The total area of the continent of Asia is approximately 45 million sq km. Calculate the percentage of land area affected by desertification using your answer to question (iii) above.

_____

v) How many cubic kilometre (cu km) of ice is lost annually from the Greenland ice cap?

_____

vi) What percentage of the USA is affected by desertification?

_____

vii) Using the World environmental issues map on pages 100–101 and the World physical map on pages 94–95, name the deserts at risk of increasing in size due to climate change and desertification that are found in the following places.

North Africa

_____

South Africa

_____

Asia

_____

Australia

_____

viii) Which country in the Caribbean is severely affected by deforestation?

_____

g) Organise the following statements into a logical order to explain how deforestation and climate change are linked. Write numbers from 1 to 4 on the lines to show the correct order for each sentence. Re-read the statements in the order you think is correct to see if it sounds sensible.

i) Deforestation and carbon dioxide

This means that carbon dioxide builds up in the atmosphere and since it is a greenhouse gas it causes the Earth's temperature to rise by helping to trap more heat on the Earth. _____

Forests are natural carbon sinks because trees absorb carbon dioxide into their leaves from the atmosphere. _____

Therefore, as humans burn more fossil fuels, not only is more carbon dioxide being produced, but when we clear forests, humans are also making it more difficult for the Earth to remove the carbon dioxide naturally. _____

This carbon dioxide is combined with water absorbed from the soil by the tree's roots to make food for the tree, in a process called photosynthesis. _____

ii) Deforestation and the water cycle

This means that rainfall is also significant because water vapour in the air forms clouds. As forests are cleared, humans limit how much water can enter the atmosphere via transpiration. _____

Trees are an important part of the water cycle. The water cycle tells us how water changes its location and state as it moves around the planet.

_____

Trees absorb liquid water from the ground and release it as water vapour into the air in a process called transpiration. Therefore, areas with large forests, especially in the tropics, have a high level of water vapour in the air.

_____

This can cause harmful conditions such as drought to occur, which in turn negatively affects agriculture and influences desertification.

_____

2 **Examine the Jamaican landscapes on page 25 of the** *Social Studies Atlas for Jamaica*. **For each landscape listed below predict the possible effects of climate change and describe one way these effects may be mitigated.**

a)   coastal plains

_____

_____

_____

_____

b)   rivers and valleys

_____

_____

_____

_____

c)   urban areas

_____

_____

_____

_____

3 Extended Learning: carbon footprint assessment

Each individual has what is called a *carbon footprint,* which is determined by their daily activities and the amount of carbon dioxide released into the atmosphere as a result. There are many online tools that can help us to calculate our carbon footprints. These are usually in the form of questionnaires asking about your daily activities. Then, based on averages from the country where you live, an overall figure is calculated for you.

Work with your class teacher to calculate your carbon footprint using an online carbon footprint calculator. Compare your results with those of your classmates and the national average for Jamaica.

Discuss as a class: what you learnt from this exercise about how much you contribute to climate change; if any of the questions were surprising for you or made you think differently about the things you do every day; how you could reduce your carbon footprint.

4 Extended Learning: global climate change monitoring

Research these organisations and agreements that are concerned with monitoring climate change. For each write:

i)   the mission statement or goal

ii)   when it was set up or ratified

iii)   which countries are members or signatories

Kyoto Protocol

Paris Agreement

The Intergovernmental Panel on Climate Change (IPCC)

Climate Action Network (CAN)

World Meteorological Organization (WMO)

Grade 8 – Term 3, Unit 2

In this unit you will learn about the different natural hazards that affect the Caribbean and some of the disaster events the region has experienced.

Caribbean geography means that the region is vulnerable to earthquakes, volcanoes and hurricanes. As such, disaster preparedness in the region includes mitigation for each of these natural hazards to reduce the disastrous impact on human life and property. A study and understanding of how past events were effectively or ineffectively managed is often a very useful tool for improving disaster management in the future. There are national and regional organisations responsible for making assessments and for monitoring and sharing information to ensure that members of the public are kept safe so the impact of these hazards is not significant.

1 Use the *Collins Jamaican School Dictionary*, pages 98 and 99 of the *Social Studies Atlas for Jamaica* and other sources to define the following terms.

a) hazard

_____

b) disaster

_____

c) drought

_____

d) flood

_____

e) earthquake

_____

f) volcanic eruption

_____

g) preparedness

_____

h) natural disaster

_____

i) storm

_____

j) hurricane

_____

k) man-made disaster

_____

l) mitigation

_____

m) vulnerable

_____

2 Read page 15 of the *Social Studies Atlas for Jamaica* to complete the following exercise.

a) Where do hurricanes affecting the Caribbean usually originate?

_____

b) What is the typical direction of movement for hurricanes in the region?

_____

c) What hazards associated with hurricanes are more likely to affect mountainous islands?

_____

d) What hazards associated with hurricanes are more likely to affect flatter islands?

_____

e) Describe weather conditions as a hurricane approaches.

_____

_____

f) Describe weather conditions close to the centre of the hurricane.

_____

_____

g) Describe weather conditions in the eye of the hurricane.

_____

_____

h) Describe weather conditions just after the eye of the hurricane has passed.

_____

_____

i) Name the months across which the hurricane season extends.

_____

j) Based on the hurricane tracks map, name those territories that are least threatened by hurricanes.

_____

k) Complete the map below by plotting the hurricane tracks of all the category 5 hurricanes in the table on page 15 of the *Social Studies Atlas for Jamaica*. Include labels and a key.

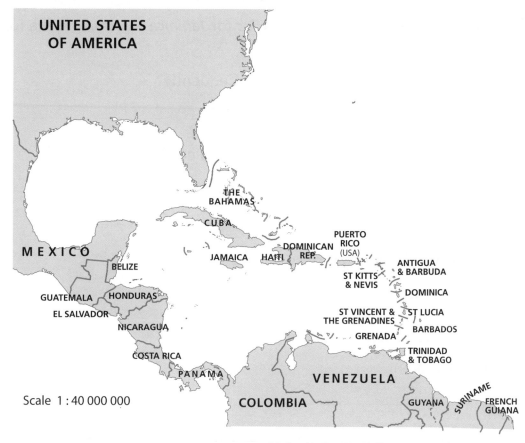

Scale 1 : 40 000 000

l) Draw a pie chart to capture the categories of recent hurricanes that have affected the region since 2004 (see the table on Recent hurricanes on page 15 of the *Social Studies Atlas for Jamaica*).

3 **Read page 16 of the *Social Studies Atlas for Jamaica* to complete the following exercise.**

a)   Where do earthquakes occur most frequently?

_____

b)   Why are Caribbean islands vulnerable to earthquakes?

_____

_____

c)   Define the following terms:

i)   epicentre

_____

ii)   focal point

_____

d)   Complete the map on the next page by:

i)   inserting the plate boundaries for the Caribbean plate

ii)   adding the arrows to show plate movement

iii)   labelling the crustal plates

iv)   shading the general earthquake zone and areas of frequent strong earthquakes

v)   labelling the locations of earthquakes with 5.0 magnitude and greater since 1900

4 Read page 17 of the *Social Studies Atlas for Jamaica* to complete the following exercise.

a) Name the plate boundaries along which volcanic activity occurs in the Caribbean.

_____

b) Describe how a subduction zone is formed.

_____

c) Explain the way many of the Caribbean islands were formed.

_____

d) State the name and location of the three extinct volcanoes in the eastern Caribbean.

_____

e) State the name and location of the active volcanoes in the eastern Caribbean.

_____

f) Label the diagram of a volcano below.

5 **Use the tables of 'Recent hurricanes' page 15, 'Major earthquakes' page 16 and 'Volcanic eruptions' page 17 of the *Social Studies Atlas for Jamaica* to complete the following exercise.**

a) **i)** Which hurricane in 2004 resulted in a higher number of deaths in the USA?

_____

ii) Suggest the possible reason for this, based on the information in the table.

_____

_____

b) **i)** In 2005, which category 4 hurricane resulted in the most loss of life in Haiti?

_____

ii) Use the 'hurricane tracks' map to offer a possible explanation for this.

_____

_____

c) In 2016, Hurricane Matthew caused significantly more deaths in Haiti than in the other countries affected. Provide two possible explanations for this.

_____

_____

_____

d) In what year and at what magnitude did major earthquakes affect Jamaica?

_____

e) In what year and at what location were the two major 8.1 magnitude earthquakes in the region?

_____

f) Complete the timeline to represent the occurrence of major earthquakes since 1900. Include the location and magnitude of the earthquakes.

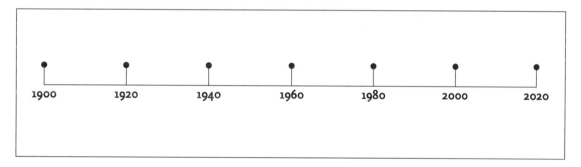

g) Construct a timeline to represent the occurrence of volcanic eruptions in the table on page 17 of the *Social Studies Atlas for Jamaica*. Include the minor eruptions and volcano name and location on your timeline.

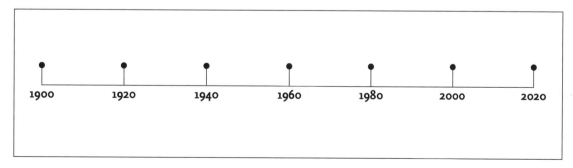

6 Extended Learning: carry out some research to write a case study on the Office of Disaster Preparedness and Emergency Management (ODPEM):

    i) describe its history and current organisational structure and important staff

    ii) its role and how it operates to meet its goals

    iii) discuss why you think organisations like the ODPEM are important

7 Extended Learning: disaster preparedness – work as a class or in groups to create a hurricane preparedness checklist and an earthquake preparedness checklist that you can use to assess your level of preparedness at home. Check online to help you determine what your checklist should include. Pay attention to:

    i) things that should be in order before a disaster

    ii) what actions should be taken during a disaster

    iii) preparation for immediately after a disaster

    iv) long-term recovery

You may also assess your school using the same checklist and present your findings.

G8 Environmental problems and solutions

Grade 8 – Term 3, Unit 3

In this unit you will learn about the environmental issues related to ecosystems.

An ecosystem is a delicate balance of abiotic cycles and biotic life cycles. Each has a role to play in keeping the ecosystem alive. Understanding how these cycles are related is essential for using the resources present sustainably and without destroying the environment.

1 Use the *Collins Jamaican School Dictionary* and other sources to define the following terms.

a) biodiversity

_____

b) habitat

_____

c) ecosystem

_____

d) conservation

_____

e) preservation

_____

f) extinction

_____

g) deforestation

_____

h) afforestation

_____

i) desertification

_____

j) endemic species

_____

k) endangered species

_____

l) environmental steward

_____

m) national park

_____

n) protected area

_____

2 **Examine each image below to complete the exercise. Circle the correct answer for each set of choices.**

a)

i) The best way to describe the type of ecosystem shown is:

aquatic　　　　　　　　　coastal　　　　　　　　　terrestrial

ii) The topography in the foreground of the image can best be described as:

flat, grassy plain　　　　mountainous forest　　　　flat, rocky desert

iii) The topography in the background of the image can best be described as:

flat, grassy plain　　　　mountainous forest　　　　flat, rocky desert

iv) List some of the components of this ecosystem.

_____

v) Describe how human activity may negatively affect this ecosystem.

_____

vi) Describe how this ecosystem may be protected.

_____

b)

i) The best way to describe the type of ecosystem shown is:

marine, coral reef　　　aquatic, lake　　　　　　terrestrial, glacier

ii) List some of the components of this ecosystem.

_____

iii) Describe some of the natural changes in this ecosystem during the course of the day.

_____

_____

iv) Describe how humans benefit from this ecosystem.

_____

_____

v) Describe how human activity may negatively affect this ecosystem.

_____

_____

vi) Describe how this ecosystem may be protected.

_____

_____

c)

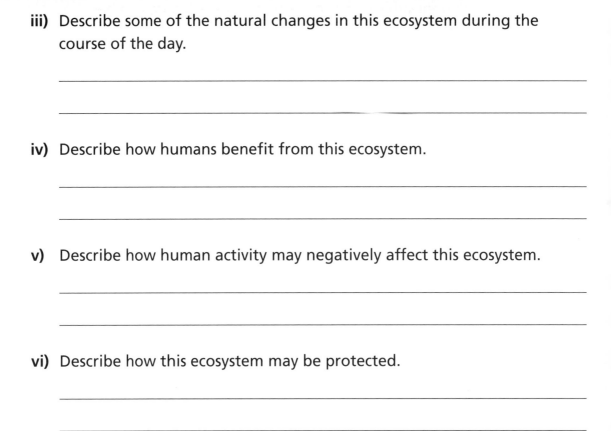

i) The best way to describe the type of ecosystem shown is:

coral reef   river valley   desert

ii) List some of the components of this ecosystem.

_____

iii) Describe the natural changes that may occur in this ecosystem over the course of a year.

_____

_____

iv) Describe how humans may benefit from this ecosystem.

_____

_____

v) Describe how human activity may harm this ecosystem.

_____

_____

vi) Describe how humans can use this ecosystem sustainably.

_____

_____

d)

i) The best way to describe the type of ecosystem shown is:

terrestrial, forest   terrestrial, grassland   marine, forest

ii) List some of the components of this ecosystem.

_____

iii) Describe how humans may use resources from this ecosystem.

_____

_____

iv) Explain two reasons why this type of ecosystem is important to life on the planet.

_____

_____

_____

_____

v) Describe how human activity may harm this ecosystem.

_____

_____

vi) Describe how humans can preserve this type of ecosystem.

_____

_____

3 Examine the image at the bottom of page 12 of the *Social Studies Atlas for Jamaica* of a mangrove wetland ecosystem. Discuss how removing the mangrove trees would:

a) directly affect the biotic components of the wetland ecosystem

_____

_____

_____

_____

b) directly affect the abiotic components of the wetland ecosystem

_____

_____

_____

_____

c) indirectly affect the biotic components of marine ecosystems beyond the wetland ecosystem

_____

_____

_____

_____

d) indirectly affect the abiotic components of marine ecosystems beyond the wetland ecosystem

_____

_____

_____

_____

4 **Select one of the environmental issues on pages 22–23 of the _Social Studies Atlas for Jamaica_. Do additional research on your selected issue to complete the following exercise.**

a) What issue did you select?

_____

b) Explain what factors may have caused or contributed to this environmental issue.

_____

_____

_____

_____

c) Explain the negative effects this issue may have on the environment.

_____

_____

_____

_____

d) Describe a Caribbean example of this issue.

_____

_____

_____

_____

e) Describe an international example of this issue.

_____

_____

_____

_____

f) Detail possible solutions for this issue.

_____

_____

_____

_____

5 Read the paragraph on endangered species on page 36 of the *Social Studies Atlas for Jamaica*. Discuss why biodiversity is important for Jamaica in terms of:

a) social life and feelings of fulfilment

_____

_____

_____

_____

b) scientific research and medicine

_____

_____

_____

_____

c) agriculture and food security

_____

_____

_____

_____

d) tourism

_____

_____

_____

_____

6 **Extended Learning: activity – ecology field study. Work with your teacher and classmates to carry out a simple field study. Use the outline below to guide you.**

Ecosystem Study

Aims: 1. To identify and describe the components of an ecosystem in the local environment.
2. To investigate the impact of human activities on the ecosystem.

Task 1: Describe the ecosystem being studied (type of ecosystem, size, etc.) and make a sketch to show its location

_____

_____

Location of ecosystem

Task 2: Describe the abiotic elements of the ecosystem

a) Does the area receive a lot of sunlight? About how many hours of sunlight?

_____

b) What is the soil like in the area (colour, texture, composition)?

_____

_____

c) Does the area receive a lot of rainfall?

_____

_____

Task 3: What are the different biotic elements in the ecosystem (plants, birds, insects, animals)?

a) For each of the biotic elements observed, identify the different types and record their numbers.

Biotic elements	Types	Count
Plants	Mango tree, hibiscus, plant, etc.	

b) Draw a simple bar graph to show the quantity for each category of biotic element.

c) Draw a diagram of a simple food chain or food web using the biotic elements observed in the ecosystem.

Task 4: In what way is the ecosystem being affected by human activity? (Pollution, concrete structures, etc.)

_____

_____

_____

_____

_____

Conclusion

_____

_____

_____

_____

_____

7 **Extended Learning: carry out some research to write a case study on the National Environmental Protection Agency (NEPA).**

a) Describe its history and current organisational structure and important staff.

b) Explain its role and how it operates to meet its goals.

c) Describe any past, present or future NEPA projects and the impact, progress or projected results of these projects.

d) Discuss why you think organisations like the NEPA are important.

Grade 9 – Term 1, Unit 1

In this unit you will learn about historical and contemporary influences on Jamaican/Caribbean culture and the spread of Jamaican/Caribbean culture around the world.

Mass media, migration and globalisation of trade and talent have contributed to the spread of cultures all over the world. Jamaican/Caribbean culture has similarly been influenced and disseminated by these forces, and with this influence, cultural preservation has become important for maintaining a strong sense of national/regional identity and pride.

1 Use the *Collins Jamaican School Dictionary* and other sources to define the following terms.

a)   culture

_____

b)   heritage

_____

c)   globalisation

_____

d)   technology

_____

e)   socialisation

_____

f)   tradition

_____

2 Jamaica and other countries of the Caribbean are multicultural societies. This means that over their history a variety of ethnic groups have settled in the region and brought with them their cultural identities, which then mixed to create what we now identify as Jamaican/Caribbean culture.

Complete the world map by adding arrows, labels and information boxes to show different parts of the world where aspects of Jamaican/Caribbean culture have originated. Try to be as specific as possible: your information boxes should be placed over the country that the aspect of culture came from and should include a description of the aspect(s) of culture being identified.

Add an appropriate title to your map.

3 Jamaican/Caribbean culture has spread to various parts of the world and has influenced communities and cultures internationally. Complete the world map by adding arrows, labels and information boxes to show the location of communities or places (at least 10) where Jamaican/Caribbean culture has had a significant influence. Include information on specific examples that can be found in these places. For example, *Grooving in the Park* concert, New York and *Rototom Sunsplash*, Spain.

Add an appropriate title to your map.

4 **Examine page 21 of the *Social Studies Atlas for Jamaica* to complete the exercise.**

a) List five places that Caribbean people have emigrated to.

_____

b) Describe two reasons why Caribbean people emigrated from the Caribbean to different countries.

_____

_____

_____

_____

c) Explain why emigration caused a spread of Caribbean culture.

_____

_____

d) Describe two ways in which Caribbean culture has spread other than emigration.

_____

_____

_____

_____

5 **Examine 'Famous Jamaicans' on page 43 of the *Social Studies Atlas for Jamaica* to complete the exercise.**

a) Explain how the success of Jamaican athletes has contributed to the following:

i) Jamaica's social development

_____

_____

_____

ii)   Jamaica's economic development

_____

_____

_____

b)   Explain how the success of Jamaican creative artists has contributed to the following:

i)   Jamaica's social development

_____

_____

_____

ii)   Jamaica's economic development

_____

_____

_____

6   **Extended Learning: preserving Caribbean and Jamaican culture. Carry out some research into examples (at least five) of how Caribbean or Jamaican culture has been lost or harmed. Describe why it is important for Caribbean and Jamaican cultural identity to be protected. Describe some ways that you think Caribbean and Jamaican culture can be protected.**

Grade 9 – Term 1, Unit 2

In this unit you will learn about past attempts at regional integration and the current state of regional integration efforts.

The Caribbean is a small geographical region with even smaller islands. In the global context, this can be a hindrance when competing with larger economies and countries of great influence. **Regional integration** has been useful to Caribbean countries by allowing them to unite and cooperate with each other to reap economic, social and political benefits. Regional integration is even more important today as **globalisation** continues to influence matters of international trade and as humans encounter more serious social and environmental issues.

1 Use the *Collins Jamaican School Dictionary* and other sources to define the following terms.

a) regional integration

_____

b) federation

_____

c) Caribbean citizen

_____

d) bilateral agreement

_____

e) multilateral agreement

_____

138

2 Examine page 45 of the *Social Studies Atlas for Jamaica* to complete the following exercise on examples of regional integration in the region.

a) Complete the table below.

Acronym	Meaning	Member states	When established	Purpose of organisation
CARICOM				
CARIFTA				
OECS				

b) List the countries that are members of CARICOM but not CARIFTA.

_____

_____

c) State one reason why a country may be a member of CARICOM but not CARIFTA.

_____

_____

3 Examine the timeline on page 42 and the map on page 45 of the *Social Studies Atlas for Jamaica* to create a timeline showing the stages of regional integration. Carry out some research to include the dates of independence of the countries involved in the Federation of the West Indies on your timeline and when the Federation of the West Indies, the region's first attempt at integration, was formed.

4 **Review other sources to complete the following exercise on entities that have been created because of regional integration.**

a) Complete the table below.

Acronym	Meaning	Area in which the Caribbean benefits from the organisation (education, health, law, etc.)	Role/purpose
UWI			
CXC			
CDEMA			
CCJ			
CARPHA			

b) Complete the map below by labelling the locations of the headquarters of CXC, UWI, CDEMA, CCJ, CARPHA and CARIFTA.

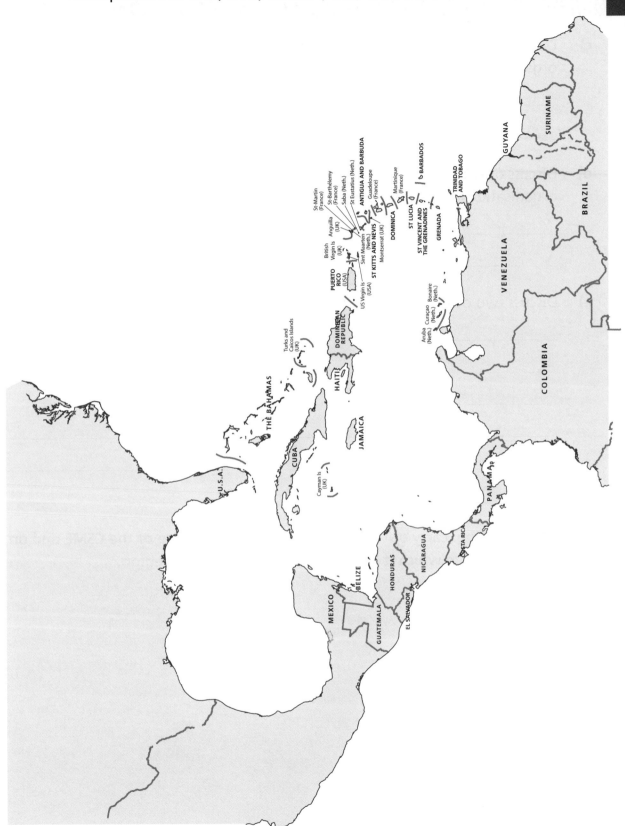

c) Discuss one advantage of having headquarters for regional integration organisations spread out across the region.

_____

_____

d) Discuss one disadvantage of having headquarters for regional integration organisations spread out across the region.

_____

_____

e) Discuss two other challenges to regional integration.

_____

_____

_____

_____

_____

_____

5 Extended Learning: carry out some research on the purpose of the CSME and on examples of ways in which it benefits people living in the region.

Grade 9 – Term 1, Unit 3

In this unit you will learn about the causes and consequences of social problems in Jamaica.

Social problems arise in every society. The exact nature of those problems is usually a result of different factors, some of which stem from historical experiences. This is the case with some of the social problems in Jamaica that have roots in the colonial history of the island, which promoted inequality based on race and class. Other factors may include changes in culture and the influence of technology. An understanding of these factors will help us to better manage these social problems and reduce the impact they have on Jamaican society.

1 Use the *Collins Jamaican School Dictionary* and other sources to define the following terms.

a) social problem

_____

b) child abuse

_____

c) domestic violence

_____

d) juvenile delinquency

_____

e) human trafficking

_____

f) poverty

_____

g) crime

_____

h) teenage pregnancy

_____

i) sexually transmitted infection

_____

2 Examine page 43 of the *Social Studies Atlas for Jamaica* and use the information on National Heroes to identify three social problems. Describe each problem using evidence from the information in the atlas and other sources, and then conclude by determining if the problem still exists in Jamaica today, explaining your response.

a) _____

_____

_____

_____

_____

_____

_____

_____

_____

_____

b) _____

_____

_____

_____

_____

c) _____

3 Examine the information and graph on AIDS/HIV on page 41 of the *Social Studies Atlas for Jamaica*. Use this information as well as other research to complete a case study on AIDS/HIV as a social issue in Jamaica. Insert statistics where possible.

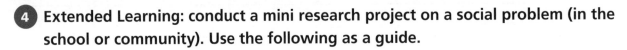

4 Extended Learning: conduct a mini research project on a social problem (in the school or community). Use the following as a guide.

    i)   Identify the problem and write your topic in the form of a question (for example: 'What are the main factors influencing students to skip classes at my school?')

    ii)   Explain why you are interested in the topic or problem you identified.

    iii)   Outline how you intend to gather the information you need and why you will be using that method (some methods include interviews and questionnaires). Also identify your target group, the number of people who will be involved and why.

    iv)   Put together at least five questions you will use for the interview or questionnaire and use them to collect the information you need.

    v)   Report the findings from the interview or questionnaire. You may use tables, graphs and descriptive paragraphs for your report.

    vi)   Draw conclusions from what you discovered.

5 Extended Learning: research the strategies implemented by the government of Jamaica to address ANY TWO of the following social issues: poverty, drug abuse, unemployment, crime.

Describe these strategies and how they were intended to solve the social problem they targeted. Assess the success of these strategies and suggest improvements for the future.

Grade 9 – Term 2, Unit 1

In this unit you will learn about Jamaican and regional development as assessed by the United Nations.

The level of **development** in a country tells us how well a country is doing socially and economically. Measuring development is an ongoing process as society changes and there is always room for improvement. The factors used when measuring development can be categorised as **economic, social, political** and **environmental**. These factors are closely related and cannot stand separately when looking at development.

1 **a)** Use the *Collins Jamaican School Dictionary* and other sources to complete the concept map below by filling in the definitions of the terms in each box.

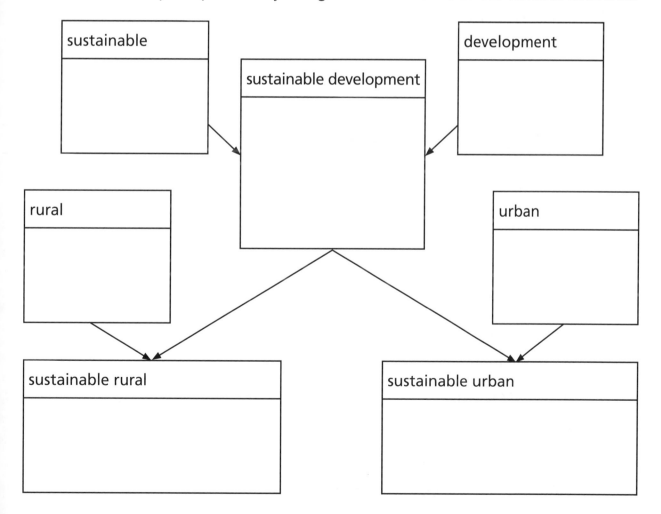

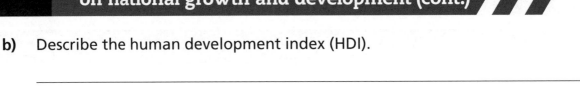

G9 Development and use of resources: impact on national growth and development (cont.)

b) Describe the human development index (HDI).

_____

_____

c) Define a country's gross national product (GNP).

_____

d) Define a country's gross domestic product (GDP).

_____

e) Explain the difference between GDP and GNP.

_____

f) Define GDP per capita and how it is calculated.

_____

2 **a)** Carry out some research and use the _Social Studies Atlas for Jamaica_ to complete the map of the Caribbean on the next page by annotating it with information boxes for ANY FIVE of the countries in the box.

Barbados	Haiti	Cuba	Trinidad and Tobago
Antigua and Barbuda	Belize	The Bahamas	Grenada

Your information box for each country should include:

i) the most recent HDI score and ranking

ii) GDP and/or GNP

iii) gross national income (GNI) per capita

iv) population size

v) life expectancy

vi) infant mortality rate

vii) adult literacy rate

viii) government expenditure on education

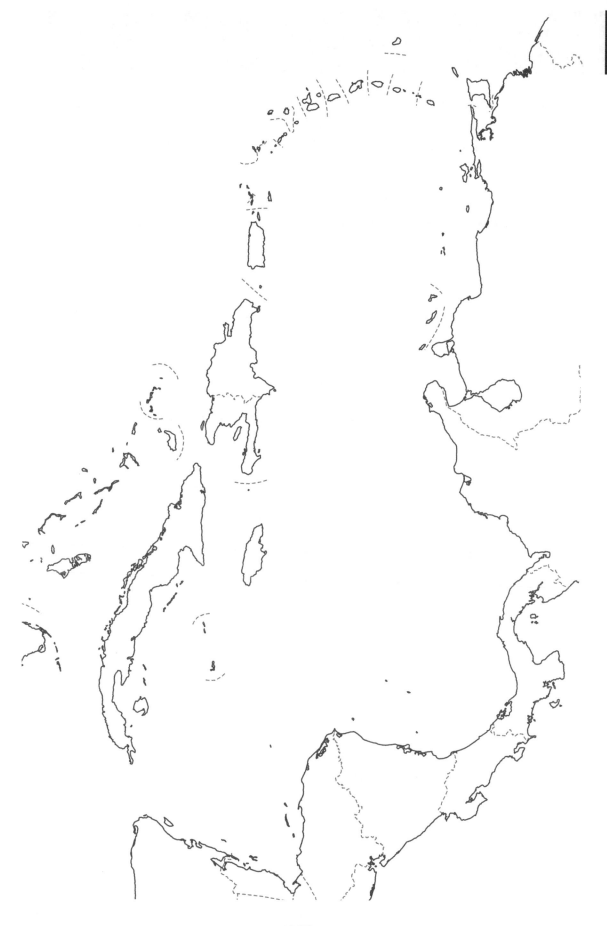

b) Consider the following questions to write an analysis of the data you have compiled on your map. Analysis includes not only answering the question but also providing reasoning behind your answer and in this case using evidence from your annotated map to support your answer. In analysis, details are key and your reasoning must be easy to follow and sensible.

i) Is there a connection between GDP/GNP and government spending on education?

_____

_____

_____

_____

ii) Is there a connection between GNI per capita and life expectancy?

_____

_____

_____

_____

iii) Is there a connection between life expectancy and infant mortality rate?

_____

_____

_____

_____

iv) Is there a connection between adult literacy rate and government spending on education?

_____

_____

_____

_____

v) Is there a connection between adult literacy rate and GNI per capita?

_____

_____

_____

_____

c) For ANY TWO countries from part 2a) write an analysis of the level of development for each country using the data you have compiled. In your analysis, include areas in which the country seems to be doing well and those areas that need improvement. Make suggestions for improving those areas.

i) Country name: _____

Analysis

_____

_____

_____

_____

_____

ii) Country name: _____

Analysis

_____

_____

_____

_____

_____

3 **a)** Carry out some research and use the *Social Studies Atlas for Jamaica* to complete the world map below by annotating it with information boxes for Jamaica and four other countries. Select from the box below.

Brazil	Canada	Germany	Nigeria
China	New Zealand	Iran	

Your information box for each country should include:

i) the most recent HDI score and ranking

ii) GDP and/or GNP

iii) gross national income (GNI) per capita

iv) population size

v) life expectancy

vi) infant mortality rate

vii) adult literacy rate

viii) government expenditure on education

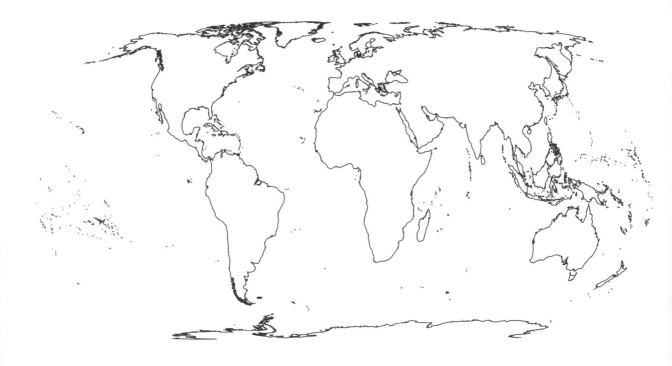

b) Compare Jamaica's development with two other countries from part 3a). Write an analysis using the data you have compiled. How well is Jamaica doing compared to these countries? What may be the reason for Jamaica doing better or worse, or the same as these countries?

    i) Jamaica vs _____

    Analysis

_____

_____

_____

_____

_____

    ii) Jamaica vs _____

    Analysis

_____

_____

_____

_____

_____

4 **a)** Examine the Government structure chart on page 24 of the *Social Studies Atlas for Jamaica* and use other sources as well to complete this exercise. Effective government is a key political factor in determining a country's overall development.

    i) Explain how each branch of government can ensure that a country develops well.

_____

_____

_____

_____

ii) Describe two things the Jamaican government has done in recent times to boost the country's development.

_____

_____

_____

_____

iii) How effective do you think these strategies have been or will be in improving Jamaica's development?

_____

_____

_____

_____

iv) Democracy is a type of government that usually ranks highly for political development. Describe what a democracy is and explain why democratic government can be useful for overall development.

_____

_____

_____

_____

v) Government corruption is harmful to a country's political development. Describe one activity that a government official may do which is corrupt, and how this may affect a country's development.

_____

_____

b) From the *Social Studies Atlas for Jamaica* examine the pages identified and respond to the questions that follow.

Economic activity, 2017 – pie chart, page 38

i) Which is the largest sector in Jamaica's economy, and which is the smallest?

_____

ii) Which sector do you believe will boost a country's level of development more? Explain your answer using examples.

_____

_____

iii) List four industries that are part of the services sector.

_____

iv) How can a strong manufacturing industry benefit the services industry? Refer to at least one of the sectors listed in your answer to question 4b(iii).

_____

_____

Jamaica Agriculture, Fishing – page 37

v) Why is agriculture important for a country's economic development?

_____

_____

vi) Using the data in the graphs, describe the performance of Jamaica's agricultural sector since the 1960s.

_____

_____

vii) What impact do you think this trend in the agricultural sector had on the country's development?

_____

_____

Jamaica Tourism – page 44

viii) Use the following key terms to describe how tourism can benefit a country's economic development.

Business tax

_____

_____

Foreign exchange

_____

_____

Employment

_____

_____

Foreign investment

_____

_____

ix) How did the tourism sector in Jamaica perform in the past 15 years?

_____

_____

c) Examine the Health statistics box on page 41 of the *Social Studies Atlas for Jamaica*.

i) Define social development.

_____

_____

ii) Explain how the health of a country's population can indicate a country's social development.

_____

_____

iii) Use the health statistics data to assess Jamaica's development. Based on the data, suggest how well Jamaica is doing. What areas need improvement?

_____

_____

_____

_____

5 **Extended Learning: review the information given on Vision 2030/National Goals in Grade 8 of this _Workbook_.**

a) Conduct research on the extent to which the National Goals are being accomplished, what has been done and what needs to be done and government plans to reach the targets by 2030.

b) Analyse what your results tell you about the future of development for Jamaica.

c) Provide feedback on positive areas of achievement and suggest improvements for areas that may be lagging behind.

Grade 9 – Term 2, Unit 2

In this unit you will learn about how the Jamaican government is structured to fulfil its role.

Jamaica is a **constitutional monarchy** with a Westminster model of government structure. In this model the administrative duties are divided across three branches: the **legislature**, the **executive** and the **judiciary**. These branches are made up of different agencies and departments, which help each arm of the government carry out its functions. It is important to understand how government is structured, its responsibility to its citizens, and the role that citizens play in ensuring the government works effectively.

1 Use the *Collins Jamaican School Dictionary* and the clues provided to complete the crossword.

Across

1. The branch of government that carries out policies and programmes
7. The parliament in a country which is responsible for making new laws
8. The system of practices and conventions that have formed the basis of the British governmental system
10. The smaller of the two houses in the legislature in some countries
11. A system of government in which the people choose their leaders by voting for them in elections
12. The group of people who govern a country

Down

1. Government department that carries out some part of the executive functions of government
2. The government departments responsible for the administration of a country
3. A formal statement of a proposed new law that is discussed and then voted on in parliament
4. The branch of government concerned with justice and the legal system
5. A law passed in parliament
6. The group of elected representatives who make the laws of a country
9. One of the rules established by a government

2 **a)** Use the 'Government structure' diagram on page 24 of the *Social Studies Atlas for Jamaica* to complete the diagram below.

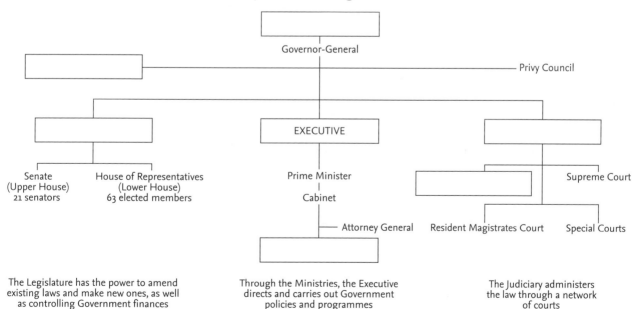

Governor-General

Privy Council

EXECUTIVE

Senate (Upper House) 21 senators
House of Representatives (Lower House) 63 elected members
Prime Minister
Cabinet
Supreme Court
Attorney General
Resident Magistrates Court
Special Courts

The Legislature has the power to amend existing laws and make new ones, as well as controlling Government finances

Through the Ministries, the Executive directs and carries out Government policies and programmes

The Judiciary administers the law through a network of courts

b) Who currently occupies the position of:

i) Monarch _____

ii) Governor-General _____

iii) Prime Minister _____

iv) Attorney General _____

v) Chief Justice _____

vi) Speaker of the House _____

vii) President of the Senate _____

c) Carry out some research to create a list of Jamaican ministries. For each ministry state the name of the current minister.

Ministry	Minister

3 **a)** Complete the following exercise on government structure.

i) What is the function of the legislative?

_____

ii) What is the function of the executive?

_____

iii) What is the function of the judiciary?

_____

iv) The act of dividing government into branches to ensure there is no overlap of roles and so that the branches remain independent of each other is common in countries with democratic governments. What is this action called?

_____

v) What is one advantage of separating the powers of the executive and the judiciary?

_____

_____

vi) What is one advantage of separating the powers of the legislature and the executive?

_____

_____

vii) What is one advantage of separating the powers of the legislature and the judiciary?

_____

_____

viii) What is one disadvantage of separation of powers?

_____

_____

b) Separation of powers and checks and balances

i) Carry out some research and write a short paragraph on the concept of _checks and balances_ in government.

_____

_____

_____

_____

_____

ii) Other than the structure of government, describe one example of a *checks and balances* system.

_____

_____

iii) Use your knowledge of the functions of each government branch to describe two examples of how separation of powers across the three branches allows *checks and balances* in the government's structure.

_____

_____

_____

_____

iv) Describe what you think would be the consequences if:

the legislature and the judiciary were combined

_____

_____

the judiciary were removed

_____

_____

the Prime Minister headed all three branches of government

_____

_____

there were no Court of Appeal

_____

_____

the legislature were removed

_____

_____

4 **Extended Learning: passing a law – draft a bill regarding a law that you would like to see passed for Jamaica. Carry out some research to describe the process that must be followed for your bill to be passed into law.**

Grade 9 – Term 2, Unit 3

In this unit you will learn about the electoral process in Jamaica.

In countries with democratic governments, citizens vote to select officials to represent their interests. The system through which this selection is done is called the **electoral process**. An agency or office of the government is usually tasked with the responsibility of planning the steps necessary before, during and after an election. This agency is guided by the country's constitution and other laws and will work to ensure citizens can exercise their right to elect their representatives in a free and fair manner.

1 Use the *Collins Jamaican School Dictionary* and other sources to define the following terms.

a) constituency

_____

b) election

_____

c) electioneering

_____

d) gerrymandering

_____

e) first-past-the-post

_____

f) vote

_____

g) poll

_____

h) polling station

_____

i) ballot

_____

j) campaign

_____

k) political party

_____

l) universal adult suffrage

_____

2 Examine the information on counties, parishes and constituencies on page 25 of the *Social Studies Atlas for Jamaica* to complete the exercise.

a) What is the relationship between the constituencies and the House of Representatives in government?

_____

_____

b) Carry out some research to complete the map on the next page.

i) Draw the constituency boundaries.

ii) Identify the constituency in which you live.

iii) Draw the county boundaries.

iv) Colour the constituencies to show which political parties currently hold each.

v) Add a descriptive key.

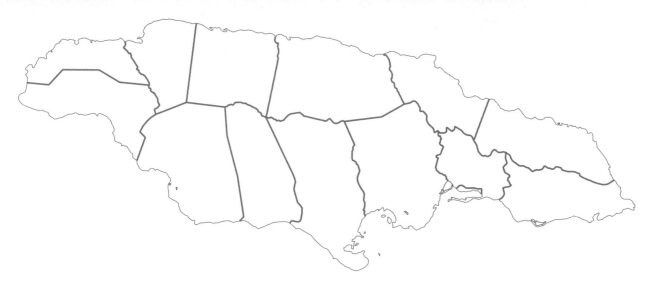

c) Respond to the questions below using your completed map.

i) Based on the map, how many representatives does each party now have in the House of Representatives?

_____

ii) Which party won most of the seats in St Catherine and St Andrew?

_____

iii) What is the total number of constituencies in each of the counties?

_____

d) Examine the parish population information in the lower table on page 40 of the *Social Studies Atlas for Jamaica*.

i) There is a correlation between the population and the number of constituencies in each parish. Describe this correlation using evidence from the *Social Studies Atlas for Jamaica*.

_____

_____

ii) Explain why you think this correlation may exist.

_____

_____

_____

_____

3 **Examine the timeline on page 42 of the _Social Studies Atlas for Jamaica_. Complete the timeline below:**

a) Annotate the events that occurred in the years shown on the timeline.

b) Label on your timeline the election years since independence.

c) Label each year with the winning party in each election. Use other sources to help with this information.

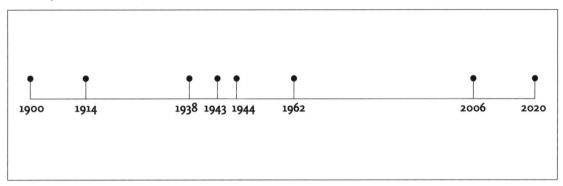

1900   1914   1938   1943   1944   1962   2006   2020

4 **Review the definition for Universal Adult Suffrage then review the timeline on page 42 of the _Social Studies Atlas for Jamaica_.**

a) What were some of the issues faced by people before Universal Adult Suffrage was granted?

_____

_____

b) Outline what you think would happen if granting Universal Adult Suffrage were reversed.

_____

_____

5 **Extended Learning: the electoral system in Jamaica.**

i) Carry out some research to find details regarding how the electoral system in Jamaica works – identify the type of electoral system and describe the steps in the electoral process.

ii) Include information about special laws or rules that govern how elections are carried out to include laws/rules about election campaigning and voting, ballot collection and counting and recounts.

iii) Research the role of the Electoral Commission of Jamaica.

iv) Critique the electoral system. Think about some of its successful features and suggest how the system could be improved.

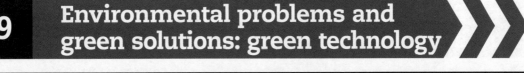
Grade 9 – Term 3, Unit 1

In this unit you will learn about environmentally friendly technology.

Technological advancements have helped to improve people's lives, but they have also helped to create some of the environmental problems that we face today. This is because we have not always taken into consideration the sustainability of the natural world. However, as the deterioration of the environment continues to make life on the planet more difficult, technological advancement has a role to play as an essential tool for overcoming some of these problems. Hence, the concept of **green technology** is becoming more prevalent and integral to the future.

1 Use the *Collins Jamaican School Dictionary* and other sources to define the following terms.

a) natural environment

_____

b) sustainable development

_____

c) green technology

_____

d) pollution

_____

e) carbon emissions

_____

f) toxic

_____

g) non-toxic

_____

h) alternative energy

_____

2 **When new technology is designed with the preservation of the natural environment in mind, it qualifies as green technology. To achieve this, green technology focuses on achieving five goals: reduce, renew, reuse/recycle, refuse and response. Complete the following exercise as we discuss these goals.**

a) **Reduce:** green technology should use less environmentally harmful fuels, water and energy as these resources should be used in quantities that will allow the technology to operate with strict efficiency.

   i) In your own words, describe what you think *reduce* as it relates to green technology means.

_____

Examine the image below and go to page 23 of the *Social Studies Atlas for Jamaica* to read the related information.

ii) Describe what is shown in the image.

_____

iii) Fossil fuels are used in many ways, especially as fuel for cars and to generate electricity. What could companies that use fossil fuels do in order to meet the _reduce_ goal of green technology?

_____

_____

iv) Explain why reducing fossil fuel use is beneficial to the natural environment.

_____

_____

v) Petroleum is one form of fossil fuel that can be used as a raw material for making new products. Identify five products that use petroleum as a raw material and explain why petroleum-based raw materials can be harmful to the environment.

_____

_____

vi) Describe how green technology can help to reduce the use of petroleum-based raw materials.

_____

_____

b) **Reuse/recycle:** green technology should recover and use existing materials in new ways. For example, some by-products viewed as waste in one process may be used as raw materials for a green technology initiative. In other cases, discarded consumer items may be repurposed or recycled for green technology projects.

i) In your own words, describe what you think _reuse and recycle_ as it relates to green technology means.

_____

_____

Examine the image below and read the related information on page 22 of the *Social Studies Atlas for Jamaica*.

ii) Describe what is shown in the image.

_____

iii) Explain how green technology that *reuses or recycles* consumer waste would prevent what is shown in the image and benefit the environment. State examples.

_____

_____

iv) Describe how consumers could be encouraged to recover their waste for *reuse or recycling* by a green technology project.

_____

_____

v) Explain how green technology that *reuses or recycles* industrial waste would benefit the environment.

_____

_____

vi) Suggest how using industrial by-products and waste instead of freshly produced raw materials may be beneficial for a green technology company.

_____

_____

c) **Renew:** green technology should use renewable energy sources.

i) Define the term renewable energy resources.

_____

Examine the image below and read the related information on page 23 of the *Social Studies Atlas for Jamaica*.

ii) Which renewable energy resource is reflected in the image?

_____

iii) Explain how using the renewable energy resource shown in the image would benefit the environment.

_____

_____

iv) As well as using wind energy, describe two other ways in which a green technology company could use renewable energy to meet its *renew* goal.

_____

_____

v) Outline one long-term benefit of using renewable energy for a green technology company.

_____

_____

d) **Refuse:** green technology should avoid the use of products that generate unnecessary waste or single-use, non-recyclable items such as plastic straws and Styrofoam™.

Examine the image below and read the related information on page 23 of the _Social Studies Atlas for Jamaica_.

i) Describe what is shown in the image and identify some threats facing these and other marine animals in the Caribbean and across the globe.

_____

_____

ii) Suggest how the _refuse_ goal can help to protect endangered species.

_____

iii) Describe ways in which the _refuse_ goal of green technology would benefit green technology companies.

_____

_____

iv) Some products that would be *refuse* are used extensively. State two examples of these products and outline what can be done to help encourage consumers and companies to refuse them.

_____

_____

v) Explain how government policies and programmes can help support the *refuse* goal of green technology.

_____

_____

e) **Response/responsibility:** the overall impact of all technological processes on the environment should be considered when using green technology. All aspects of a business, from production to sales, should be considered and responsibility taken for managing any impacts on the natural environment. Any negative impacts on the environment from using green technology should be addressed so that the 'green' status of the technology can be maintained.

i) Explain the *responsibility* goal in your own words.

_____

Examine the images here and on the next page and go to page 22 of the *Social Studies Atlas for Jamaica* to read the related information.

ii) Describe what is shown in each of the images.

_____

iii) Explain how the *response/responsibility* goal can help mitigate the problems shown in each image above.

_____

_____

iv) Explain how the *response/responsibility* goal of green technology would influence the actions of a company that discovers that mining of its raw materials causes irreversible damage to a forest.

_____

_____

v) Do you think consumers are more likely or less likely to support a responsible green technology company? Explain your answer.

_____

_____

vi) Suggest how a green technology company can use its efforts to reach its *response/responsibility* goal to boost customer loyalty.

_____

_____

3 Carry out some research on green technology projects in Jamaica. Include one hydroelectric, one solar, one wind power and one waste recycling project or initiative.

Use the information you gather to complete the map below.

i) Name/identify the type of project/company and identify the location of the project or company on the map.

ii) Add information boxes with information about the project or company such as the start-up date, the type of project it is, accomplishments (for example, the amount of electricity generated or waste removed), challenges faced by the project or company and any future plans for the project or company.

iii) Add a descriptive key.

4 Use information from the *Social Studies Atlas for Jamaica* and other sources to complete the following questions on sustainable and unsustainable practices.

a) What does the term *sustainable* mean?

_____

b) Examine the images of deforestation and water pollution on page 36 of the *Social Studies Atlas for Jamaica* and explain why the practices contributing to these issues could be considered *unsustainable*.

_____

_____

c) Suggest ways in which some of the practices contributing to the issues could be more sustainable.

_____

_____

d) Examine the Deforestation map on page 101 of the *Social Studies Atlas for Jamaica* to explore the prevalence of deforestation as an unsustainable practice worldwide.

i) Which continent had the largest decrease in forest areas between 2000 and 2010?

_____

ii) Which continent had the smallest increase in forest areas?

_____

iii) On which continent was there no change in forest areas?

_____

iv) Calculate the level of change for South America, Africa and Australia and represent the information on a bar graph.

_____

_____

_____

_____

```
┌─────────────────────────────────────────────┐
│                                             │
│                                             │
│                                             │
│                                             │
│                                             │
│                                             │
│                                             │
│                                             │
└─────────────────────────────────────────────┘
```

v) List the factors that may be contributing to the loss of forest areas on these continents.

_____

_____

_____

_____

e) One way of combating deforestation is to declare some areas as *protected forests*. Examine the graphs on page 36 of the *Social Studies Atlas for Jamaica* to complete the following questions.

i) What percentage of forests in Jamaica are 'protected'?

_____

ii) Was there any change for areas between 2009 and 2014?

_____

iii) Apart from declaring areas as protected, what else can we do to ensure forests are used sustainably?

_____

_____

_____

_____

Grade 9 – Term 3, Unit 2

In this unit you will learn about successful attitudes, actions and ethics in the workplace.

Workplace ethics involve individuals thinking and acting in a way that creates a positive working environment for all while they are carrying out their duties in the workplace. The ability to carry out a job effectively is dependent not only on technical knowledge, qualifications, experience or practical skills but also on the ability to navigate the workplace through effective and mindful communication and other qualities more commonly known as **soft skills**. Workplace ethics also involve ensuring actions do not contribute to conflict but where this is unavoidable at work, the individual may appeal to a **trade union**, which will offer advice and give support to employees to ensure the successful resolution of issues.

1 Use the *Collins Jamaican School Dictionary* and other sources to define the following terms.

a) value

_____

b) work

_____

c) work ethic

_____

d) job

_____

e) right

_____

f) responsibility

_____

g) trade union

_____

h) employer

_____

i) employee

_____

j) industrial dispute

_____

k) arbitration

_____

l) collective bargaining

_____

m) sick-out

_____

n) lock-out

_____

o) lobbying

_____

p) work to rule

_____

q) strikes

_____

r) career

_____

s) profession

_____

t) child labour

_____

2 Examine the Caribbean countries pages of the *Social Studies Atlas for Jamaica*, pages 45–72. Look at the graphics, maps and information boxes to determine ten possible careers or employment opportunities across the region. For each career you identify, name the career and state the page and graph, picture or information from the *Social Studies Atlas for Jamaica* that suggested it may be a job/career in the region. Explain your reasoning. Carry out some research about the career or job. Complete the table below to show what the career/job involves and what skills or qualifications are required.

Career	*Atlas* evidence (page, image or graph)	Description of career (roles and duties, responsibilities related to career)	Qualification/ special skills required

3 Examine the population pyramids on page 41 of the *Social Studies Atlas for Jamaica.*

a) Which age groups do you think are part of the workforce?

_____

_____

b) Why do you think it is important for a country to have a large workforce?

_____

_____

c) Estimate the percentage working population for the two years. For which of the two years was the working population larger?

_____

d) The name given to the population group outside the working population is the dependency group.

   i) Which age groups fall into this category?

   _____

   ii) What is the disadvantage of having a small working population compared to the dependent population?

   _____

   _____

e) Discuss how each of the following factors could reduce productivity, even if a country has a large working-age population:

   i) lack of education

   _____

   _____

   ii) poor health services

   _____

   _____

iii) economic depression

_____

_____

iv) poor governance

_____

_____

f) State some of the social consequences that occur when a country has high levels of unemployment.

_____

_____

4 **Examine the image of the doctor and patient on page 41 of the _Social Studies Atlas for Jamaica_.**

a) Describe three ways that the doctor would demonstrate good work ethics in his dealing with the patient.

_____

_____

_____

_____

_____

b) Are any of the things described in question 4a above relevant to other jobs and careers? Explain your response.

_____

_____

_____

_____

c) Describe two examples of good work ethics in the service industries.

_____

_____

_____

_____

d) Describe two examples of good work ethics in the manufacturing industry.

_____

_____

_____

_____

e) Describe two examples of good work ethics in the agricultural industry.

_____

_____

_____

_____

f) Explain why good work ethics are important.

_____

_____

g) For ANY TWO ethical actions you have described in this exercise, explain how they can benefit the employee, or the employer, to practise these actions.

_____

_____

_____

_____

5 Extended Learning: research the rights and responsibilities of employees in Jamaica. Use the information gathered to create an educational pamphlet for workers.

Research the role and history of trade unions in Jamaica. Create a poster to represent your findings.

Grade 9 – Term 3, Unit 3

In this unit you will learn about the tourist industry and its importance to economic development in Jamaica and the Caribbean.

Tourism has long been synonymous with the Caribbean. A combination of natural environmental factors such as an inviting climate and beautiful landscapes along with the close proximity to large markets and a diverse culture have made the Caribbean a successful tourist destination. Therefore, the importance of tourism to the development of Jamaica and the wider region must be understood, especially as globalisation has caused an increase in competition in the industry. An understanding of this connection can lead to effective strategies for promoting tourism and protecting tourism in the region.

1 Use the *Collins Jamaican School Dictionary* and other sources to complete the concept map below by filling in the definitions of the terms in each box.

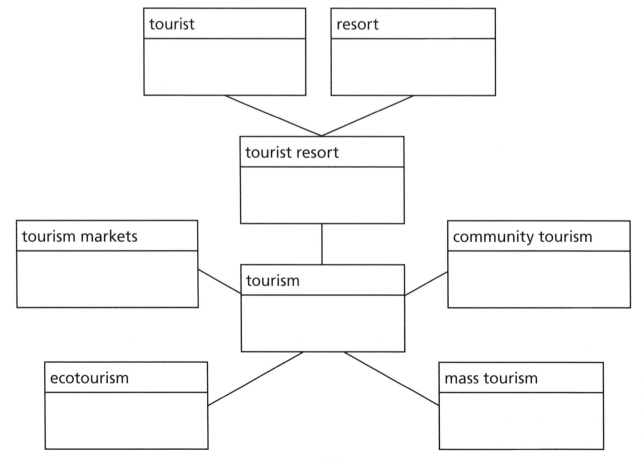

2 Examine the images on each of the following pages of the *Social Studies Atlas for Jamaica*. For each image identify the type of tourism (mass, eco, community, etc.), some jobs that are directly and/or indirectly provided by the tourism activity shown and the possible impact of the activity on the environment.

G9

a) Dunn's River Falls, St Ann (page 31)

_____

_____

_____

_____

b) Cruise ship in Montego Bay (page 32)

_____

_____

_____

_____

c) Bamboo rafting, Martha Brae River (page 44)

_____

_____

_____

_____

d) Ocho Rios (page 44)

_____

_____

_____

_____

e) *Carnival Valor*, Castries, St Lucia (page 57)

_____

_____

_____

_____

f) Front Porch, Bonaire (page 62)

_____

_____

_____

_____

g) Caroni Swamp, Trinidad (page 65)

_____

_____

_____

_____

3 Examine the Tourism Features map on page 44 of the *Social Studies Atlas for Jamaica* to complete the following exercise.

a) Name the southernmost point of interest on the map and the parish it is found in.

_____

b) What is the name of the national park shown on the map?

_____

c) How many major resorts are located in St James on the map?

_____

d) Name the two points of interest in St Elizabeth.

_____

e) In which parish is Blue Hole Mineral Spring found?

_____

f) List the parishes with cruise ship ports.

_____

g) Name the two main airports on the map.

_____

h) List all the botanical gardens on the map and for each, state the parish in which it is found.

_____

4 **Analyse the tourism graphs on page 44 to complete the exercise.**

a) **i)** From which country did most stop-over visitors come in 2016?

_____

ii) Provide one reason for this.

_____

_____

b) Of the stop-over visitors to Jamaica in 2016, 3% came from the Caribbean. Give two possible reasons why Caribbean visitors only made up this small percentage.

_____

_____

c) Outline two factors that could explain the trend in stop-over visitor arrivals from 2001 to 2016.

_____

_____

_____

_____

d) In 2016, stop-over arrivals peaked in March, July and December. Provide possible explanations for peak visitor arrivals at these times of the year.

_____

_____

e) Which purpose of visit do you think would benefit the country most? Explain your answer.

_____

_____

f) Compare the Cruise passenger arrivals, 2001–2016 graph to the Stop-over visitor arrivals, 2001–2016 graph. The cruise passenger arrivals seem to vary more from year to year. Provide a possible explanation for this observation.

_____

_____

g) During which months is the tourism industry most likely to benefit from cruise passenger arrivals?

_____

5 **Regional tourism trends**

a) Compare the Cruise passenger arrivals, 2001–2016 Jamaica graph (page 44) with the Tourist arrivals (cruise ships), 2000–2014 for the Cayman Islands (page 49). Describe any similarities observed in the trends. Provide one possible reason for any similarity observed.

_____

_____

_____

b) Compare the Stop-over visitor arrivals in Jamaica from 2009–2014 on page 44, with the stay over Tourist arrivals, 2009–2014 in St Lucia on page 57. Describe any similarity or difference in the trend during this time. Provide explanations for your observations.

_____

_____

_____

c) Compare the 2016 Stop-over visitor arrivals and the Cruise passenger arrivals by month for Jamaica (page 44), with the 2014 Stop-over visitor arrivals and the Cruise passenger arrivals by month for Trinidad and Tobago (page 67). Describe any similarities or differences in the trends observed between the graphs. Provide explanations for any observations.

_____

_____

_____

_____

_____

_____

6 **Extended Learning: carry out some research into sustainable tourism projects in Jamaica and the rest of the Caribbean.**

i) Explain what is meant by sustainable tourism.

ii) Find examples of projects or steps being taken to make tourism sustainable in the region.

iii) Analyse the results of some of these strategies as examples of success and instances for improvement.

iv) Design and provide justification for your own strategies for promoting and ensuring sustainable tourism in Jamaica and the rest of the Caribbean.

Index